Envisioning New England

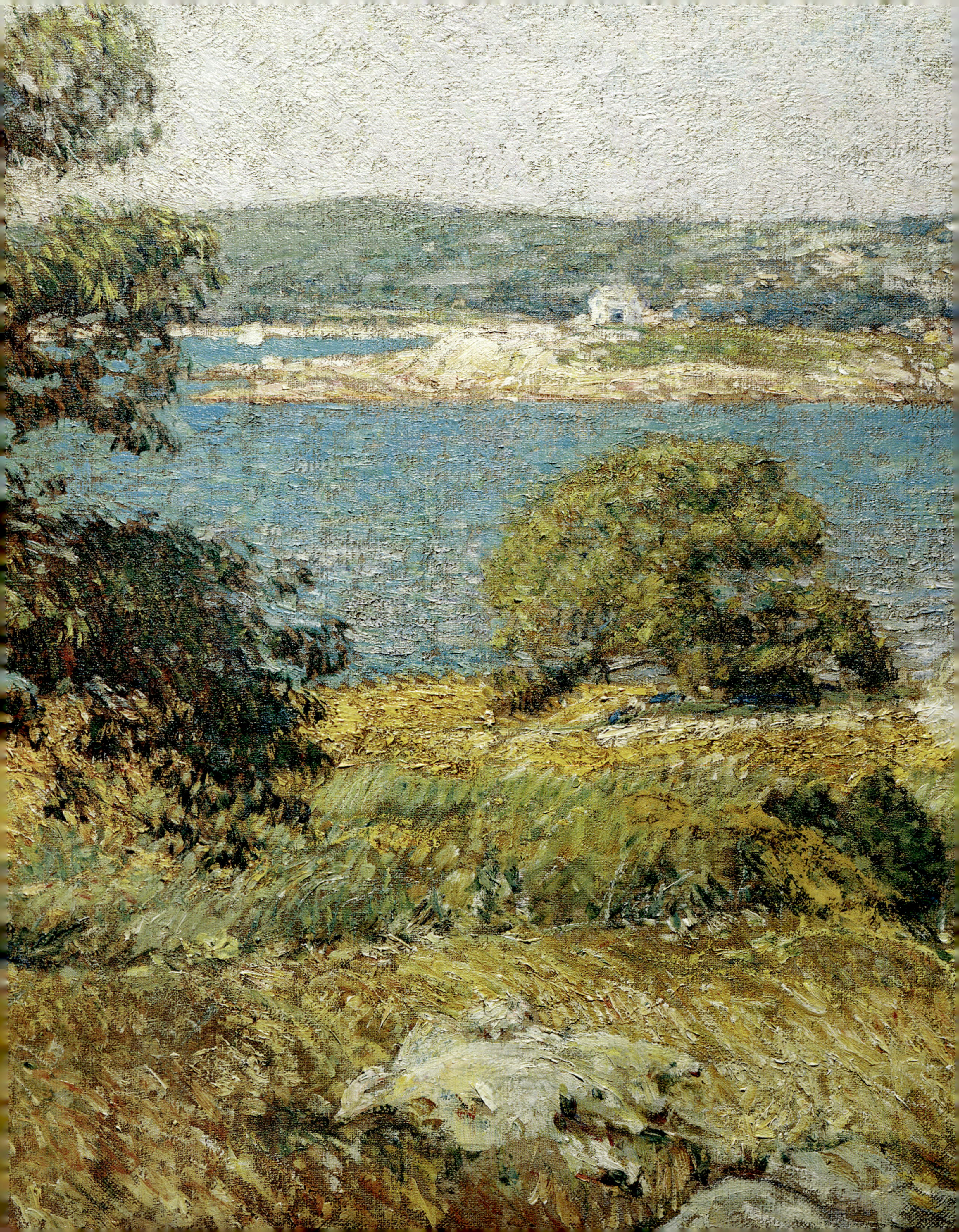

Envisioning New England

TREASURES FROM COMMUNITY ART MUSEUMS

Edited by Pamela J. Belanger

University Press of New England *Hanover and London*

IN ASSOCIATION WITH THE CONSORTIUM OF NEW ENGLAND COMMUNITY ART MUSEUMS

Published by University Press of New England,
One Court Street, Lebanon, NH 03766
In association with the Consortium of New England Community Art Museums
www.upne.com

Printed in Singapore
5 4 3 2 1
CIP data appear at the end of the book

Museum building photograph credits:

Art Complex Museum. Photograph by Stewart Clements and William Howcroft, Boston, Massachusetts. Courtesy of the Art Complex Museum.

Bennington Museum. Courtesy of the Bennington Museum, photo by Nicholas Whitman.

Cape Museum of Fine Arts. Courtesy of Polhemus Savery DaSilva Architects & Builders.

Danforth Museum of Art. Foreground, David Lang, *The Question is the Answer,* 1979. Courtesy of the Danforth Museum of Art.

Farnsworth Art Museum. Courtesy of the Farnsworth Art Museum. Photograph by Melville McLean

Fitchburg Art Museum. Courtesy of the Fitchburg Art Museum.

Florence Griswold House. Courtesy of the Florence Griswold Museum © Jeff Goldberg/Esto. All rights reserved.

The Krieble Gallery. Courtesy of the Florence Griswold Museum © Jeff Goldberg/Esto. All rights reserved.

Fruitlands Museums. Foreground, Philip Sears, *Pumunangwet,* 1931. Courtesy of Fruitlands Museums.

Fuller Museum of Art. Courtesy of Fuller Museum of Art.

Lyman Allyn Art Museum. Courtesy of the Lyman Allyn Art Museum.

Mattatuck Museum. Courtesy of the Mattatuck Museum.

New Britain Museum of American Art. Foreground, Sol LeWitt, *Complex Form #4*. Courtesy of New Britain Museum of American Art.

Newport Art Museum and Art Association. Courtesy of Newport Art Museum and Art Association.

Provincetown Art Association and Museum. Courtesy of Provincetown Art Association and Museum.

Contents

❦ *Preface*

Christine Callahan
Director, Newport Art Museum
and Art Association
President, Consortium of New
England Community Art Museums

We present this exhibition and publication with thanks to our museum visitors and colleagues who draw inspiration from art, and in appreciation of the benefactors and concerned citizens who worked so hard to build our institutions. As you read this catalogue and descriptions of the participating museums you will see that the Consortium of New England Community Art Museums is made of special places, each created by one or many people dedicated to enriching the lives of others through the sharing of artistic resources. At the core of each member museum is an outstanding art collection and a strong and enduring tie to the local community.

In 1993 fifteen community art museums in New England founded this consortium for the purpose of broadening their impact, sharing their resources, and creating an environment for collaboration. As the institutions have evolved, so too has the consortium. Today, our members number fourteen, with eleven of the original members still active participants. Each member museum grants free or reduced admission to members of other consortium institutions. A collaborative Web site (*www.communityartmuseums.org*) offers general information about the member museums and provides a link to the Web site of each individual museum. Three times a year the museum directors come together for meetings and programs of mutual interest. They work together to exchange information for the benefit of the institutions, staff, and museum visitors.

This project represents a new level of community performance for our museums—reaching out beyond their geographic home, their immediate neighbors, and their familiar patrons to a broader audience including artists, students, scholars, museum professionals, and the general public. *Envisioning New England: Treasures from Community Art Museums* represents a groundbreaking collaborative effort. The exhibition and publication offer a rare opportunity to view in one place a group of paintings that includes several masterworks by some of the most important nineteenth- and twentieth-century American artists. This project presents but a sampling of New England's rich artistic legacy and invites deeper exploration of the collections of the

Consortium's member museums. We hope that the actual exhibition and this catalogue will serve as a catalyst to explore the important collections at each participating museum. There you will find the engaging exhibitions, lectures, and programs that I hope will encourage you to participate in the artistic life of your community.

My thanks to the many hardworking professionals who helped the Consortium bring this extraordinary group of paintings to you. Without the support of the Consortium institutions and their staffs this project could not have been realized.

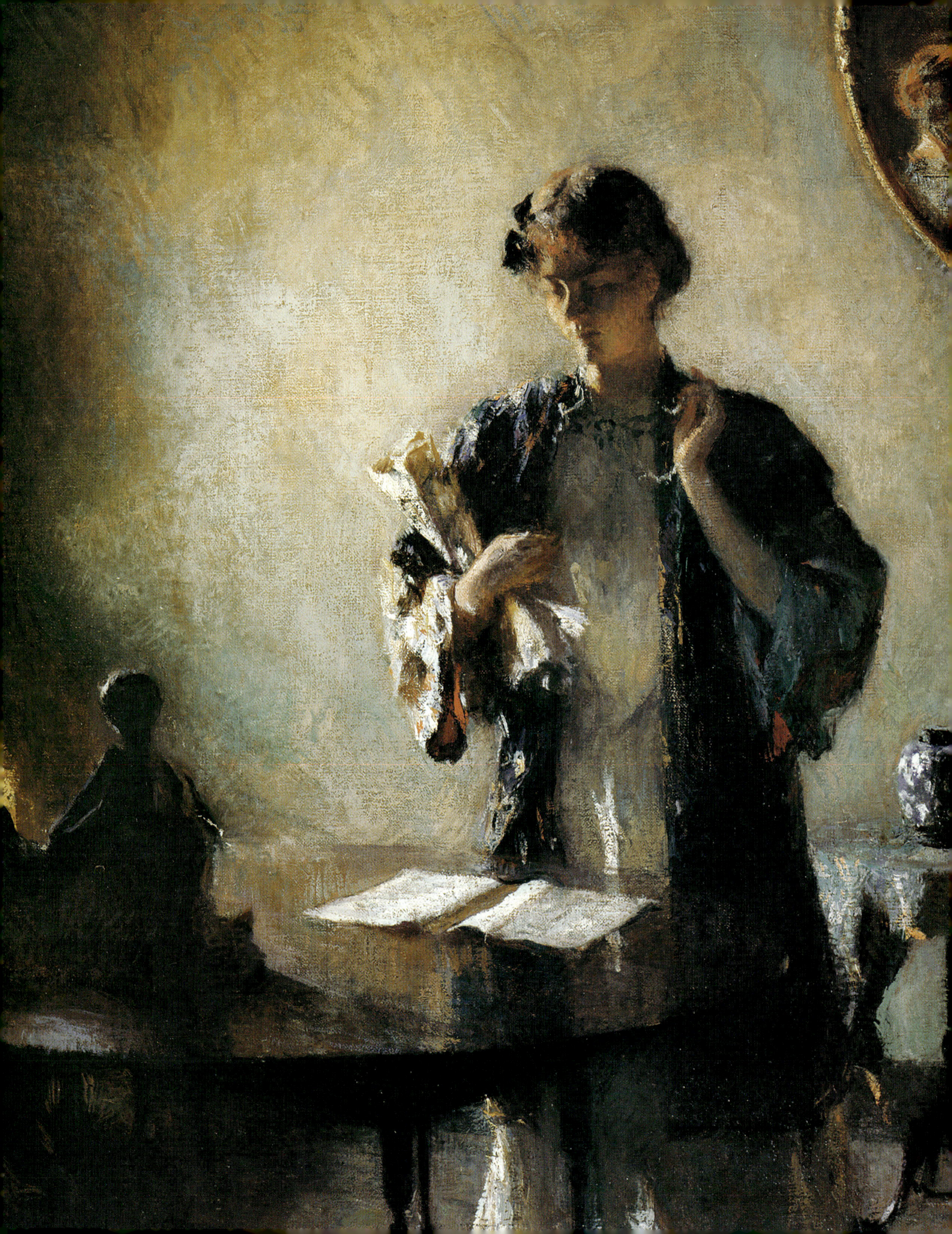

❦ *Acknowledgments*

Stephanie N. Upton
Project Director
Executive Director, Consortium of New England Community Art Museums

Envisioning New England: Treasures from Community Art Museums is truly a collaborative effort whose success rests with the unfailing dedication of the museum professionals who have made this project possible. The exhibition documented in this book was proposed in spring 2000 by Douglas Hyland, director of the New Britain Museum of American Art and, at that time, president of the Consortium of New England Community Art Museums. His proposal was quickly embraced by Jeffrey Andersen, director of the Florence Griswold Museum, who early on championed the idea of a catalogue and provided much appreciated support and guidance throughout the project. Current consortium president Christine Callahan of the Newport Art Museum has gracefully and deliberately moved the exhibition forward, listening, advising, and assisting me on numerous occasions.

The directors of Consortium museums not only nurtured the project and generously donated staff time and resources but also came together in an unbelievable way to offer their experience, expertise, and goodwill to me as the project evolved. I wish to thank our directors and former directors: Charles Weyerhaueser, Art Complex Museum; Richard Borges, Bennington Museum; Elizabeth Ives Hunter, Gregory Harper, Donald Knaub, Cape Museum of Fine Arts; Ronald Crusan, Danforth Museum of Art; Chistopher Crosman, Farnsworth Art Museum; Peter Timms, Fitchburg Art Museum; Jeffrey Andersen, Florence Griswold Museum; Maud Ayson, Fruitlands Museums; Gretchen Keyworth, Jennifer Atkinson, Fuller Museum of Art; Christopher Steiner, Charles A. Shephard III, Lyman Allyn Art Museum; Marie Galbraith, Mattatuck Museum; Douglas Hyland, New Britain Museum of American Art; Christine Callahan, Newport Art Museum; and Christine McCarthy, Provincetown Art Association and Museum.

Without the dedicated efforts of three people this book would never have been possible. The exhibition curators, Jack Becker, director of Cheekwood Museum of Art (formerly curator of the Florence Griswold Museum) and Nancy Whipple Grinnell, curator of Newport Art Museum, came to the project with strong backgrounds in American Art and a particular commitment to the artists of New England that defines *Envisioning New England*. I appreciate their willingness to give of their time and expertise in addition to the normal professional demands of their jobs and busy personal lives. They are the modern "visionaries" behind this project!

Pamela J. Belanger, independent art historian (formerly curator of collections at the Farnsworth Art Museum), assumed the enormous task of overseeing the preparation of this catalogue, serving as editor for the Consortium. We have her to thank for producing a book of such high quality. I am particularly grateful for her expertise, her patience, and her unfailing belief in this project. She, too, gave of her time and talent on top of an already demanding schedule. Throughout the process, Jack, Nancy, and Pamela worked together with me in a highly professional manner that encouraged mutual support of our best efforts—the true essence of collaboration!

The Consortium owes a debt of gratitude to William H. Truettner, senior curator of the Smithsonian Museum of American Art, whose scholarship served as an inspiration for the project. His contribution provides a rich context while acknowledging a critical goal of the project—as celebration of the art of New England and of New England's art museums.

The staff at each institution contributed in a variety of ways, providing images and information for this book and editing copy. I appreciate the careful work of so many who responded to my requests: Laura Doherty, Catherine Mayes, and Maureen Wengler, Art Complex Museum; Ruth Levin and Maryann St. John, Bennington Museum; Rory Marcus, Cape Museum of Fine Arts; Mary Margaret Sesak, Kit Stone, Angela Waldron, and Victoria Woodhull, Farnsworth Art Museum; Tom Burchell, Pamela Russell, and Mary Ellen LeTarte, Fitchburg Art Museum; Laurie Bradt, Amy Ellis, Tammi Flynn, Susie Forbes, Patty Whitman, and Nicole Wholean, Florence Griswold Museum; Michael Volmar, Fruitlands Museums; Linda Lavin, Kathleen McCleary, Lori Read, and Nancy Stula,

Lyman Allyn Art Museum; Raechel Guest, Mattatuck Museum; Paula Bender, Mel Ellis, James Kopp, Kristy Mathews, and Maura O'Shea, New Britain Museum of American Art; Gail Hargreaves, Newport Art Museum. Thanks, too, to Kirsti Blom and Jane Kallir of Grandma Moses Properties Company, and to the support staff at each institution who remain nameless but who assisted in producing images and responding to requests. I am indebted to a friend and colleague, Sarah Brophy of bMuse, for proofreading text for me.

Special thanks to Victoria Woodhull and the team of educators who assisted as they built interpretive programs, based upon the exhibition and catalogue: Roger Dell, Judith Hambleton, Kristine Hastreiter, Tina Mirto, Joanne Myers, David Rau, and Stephenie Sala.

All who worked diligently to ensure the success of this catalogue will be forever grateful to those at University Press of New England who enthusiastically embraced publishing this catalogue. We are deeply indebted to Richard Abel, Sarah Welsch, and Ellen Wicklum for their appreciation of the significance of this book, both for its own merits and as an example of collaboration. They have provided keen advice and patiently understood the intricacies of working with a consortium of fourteen museums. Thanks also to Mary Crittendon, Katherine Kimball, and Richard Pult.

To all these special people and institutions, my heartfelt thanks. *Envisioning New England* is the result of their personal and organizational commitment and represents a combined wealth of talent that is truly remarkable. I consider it a professional honor and personal joy to be associated with this project and the Consortium itself.

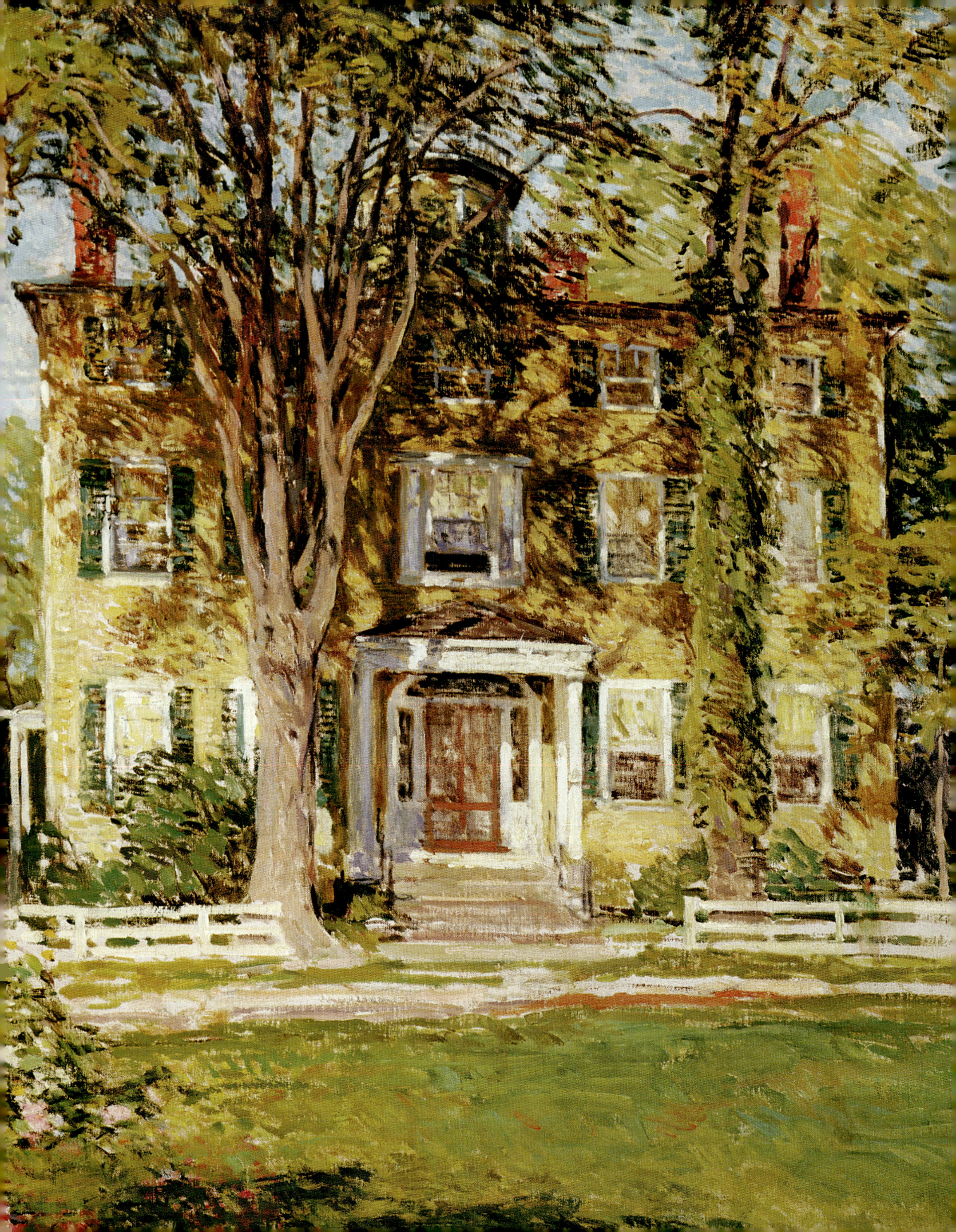

Introduction

William H. Truettner
Senior Curator, Smithsonian Museum of American Art

How one distinguishes between regional art and history museums and institutions with larger, more encyclopedic collections has never been clear, perhaps because the point at which they divide is finally a judgment call. Still, we continue to make a distinction between the two, and we often turn to regional museums to provide information that we can't get from larger institutions. Michael Kammen claims in his book *Mystic Chords of Memory* that this two-tiered system has a healthy social benefit—that regional museums work to decentralize and therefore democratize our culture. Their mission, in effect, is to break down our national story into a series of smaller stories that present a more diverse cultural map of the country. The problem with applying that theory to New England, however, is that the so-called border between regional and national has always been more porous than other regional/national borders. Indeed, for most of the years this project covers, many of the attributes of New England culture were thought to be those of the nation.

How did this happen? By the time the earliest of the museums participating in this project was founded, New England and United States history had been written and rewritten for several decades, in large part by New Englanders. The process gave New England primacy over other regions of the country; its history, and the images associated with that history, became over time the models for history-making, and as they were applied to other parts of the country, an idealized narrative about the New England colonial past was reinscribed for countless new settlements in the trans-Appalachian West, regardless of how they actually got started. By the early twentieth century, that gave New England a unique historical status—in the minds of many Americans, it had become a microcosm of the nation.

The benefit to New England cultural institutions, especially those included in this exhibition, was immediate and long lasting. A growing historical self-consciousness encouraged prosperous New Englanders to direct their philanthropy toward the founding of local institutions that in one way or another served to memorialize the region's past. Art and history museums were thought to be uniquely suited to this role, or so one concludes from the number that came into being between the 1870s and the mid–twentieth century. The collections of these museums, no matter how broad their mandate, inevitably included images associated with the New England past. At first, these images were seen in terms of their historical more than their aesthetic role, as documents that served to illustrate life in "Old New England." But gradually their combined aesthetic and historical roles were renegotiated, from documents to ideal images—or from documents to images that represented an imaginary, if still deeply revealing, past. That, in any case, is what seems to distinguish the splendid works included in this exhibition and publication.

These works, however, were not necessarily created or collected to appeal to a narrow regional audience; on the contrary, they address broad-based aesthetic and historical concerns, as broad, certainly, as the American works that were concurrently being added to the collections of larger art institutions around the country. But those institutions often chose to present these works as simply unique and beautiful, thereby obscuring the local stories they might tell. The organizers of this project, to their credit, have sought to preserve the finely textured regional nuance embodied in each of these works while still linking them to major trends in American art.

❦ Envisioning New England

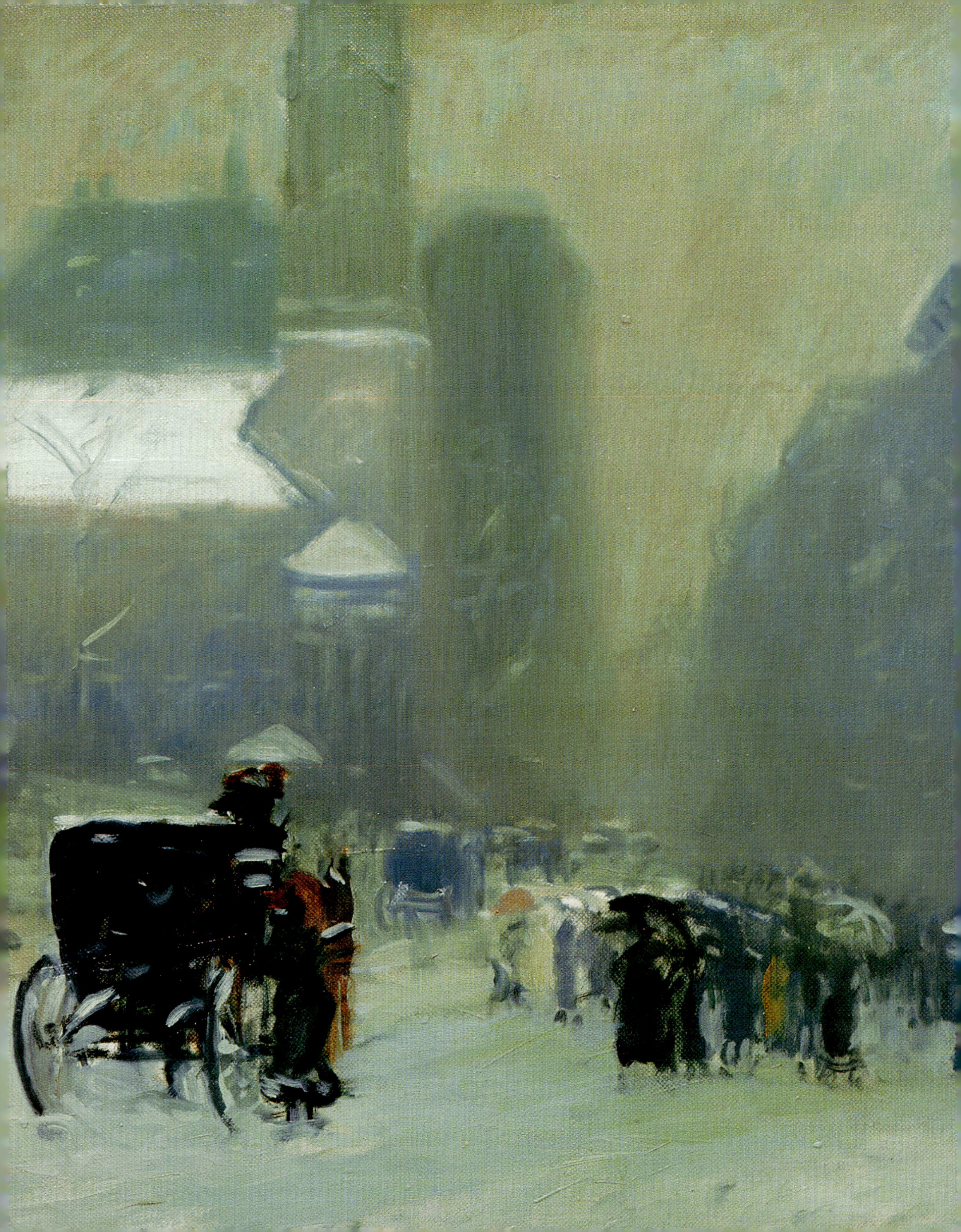

Founding Visions

The Evolution of New England's Community Art Museums

Nancy Whipple Grinnell

Curator, Newport Art Museum and Art Association

❦ THE INSTITUTIONS IN the Consortium of New England Community Art Museums have consistently shared a recognition of the capacity of art to enrich lives, whether their founders were prominent collectors, affluent citizens, or grassroots arts advocates. For some it was simply a duty of civic-mindedness. Eleanor Norcross, one of the first American women to found an art museum and endow it with works of art, established the Fitchburg Art Museum in 1927. Her father, a dedicated public servant, had instilled in her the need to give back to the community. At the time, Fitchburg was a burgeoning industrial city, and its citizens would benefit from the infusion of culture that a museum would bring. For others it was a sense of beneficence. Collectors Carl and Edith Weyerhaeuser wanted to share their world-class collection of fine art with their community, and so they established the Art Complex Museum, in Duxbury, Massachusetts, in 1971 (see figures 1, 2, 3). For still others, it was a group initiative. In 1912, in Newport, Rhode Island, inspired citizens led by author and activist Maud Howe Elliott formed the Art Association of Newport (today the Newport Art Museum and Art Association), its purpose being "the cultivation and promotion of artistic endeavor and interest in the arts."[1] Over fifty years later, in Framingham, Massachusetts, a local businessman named Paul Marks gathered together a handful of dedicated citizens in his living room, and the Danforth Museum of Art was born.

Sometimes art appreciation was not a catalyst, but the result of the merging of art and history. It was a historical event, the 1777 Battle of

Bennington, that galvanized the Bennington Historical Society in Vermont to organize in 1875, but significant early acquisitions of painting and sculpture by regional artists expanded the organization's vision. Today the Bennington Museum houses the largest public collection of Grandma Moses's paintings and memorabilia, among other treasures (see figure 44). The Mattatuck Museum in Waterbury, Connecticut, began as the Mattauck Historical Society in 1877 (see figures 50, 51). By 1900 it was incorporated "to collect and preserve whatever may serve to explain or illustrate the archaeology, the art, the literature, the history civil, ecclesiastical or natural of the state of Connecticut, and especially that part thereof which was anciently known as Mattatuck." With such verbiage, regional museums came into being.

Collecting and exhibiting artworks provided the impetus for the growth and development of other New England community museums. In the first half of the twentieth century, while the Western art world was embroiled in debates over modern art versus traditional work, the participants in New England's developing museum scene addressed and refined their collecting goals. Nowhere was the controversy more prevalent than at the Provincetown Art Association and Museum, in Massachusetts. It was founded in 1914 to "promote and cultivate the practice and appreciation of all branches of the fine arts, to assemble and maintain in the town of Provincetown and environs a collection of works of art of merit." The Impressionist establishment in Provincetown, with Charles Webster Hawthorne in the forefront (see figure 4), did not take kindly to modernist interlopers. A lively debate ensued, and compromise was reached by alternating exhibitions. No contest occurred at the Florence Griswold Museum in Old Lyme, Connecticut, which had its beginnings as an art colony devoted to the American Barbizon and emerged as a center of American Impressionism (see figure 5). The artistic creativity and camaraderie sustained by "Miss Florence" still permeates the historic Griswold House. At the New Britain Museum of American Art, in Connecticut, founded in 1903 as the first museum with that

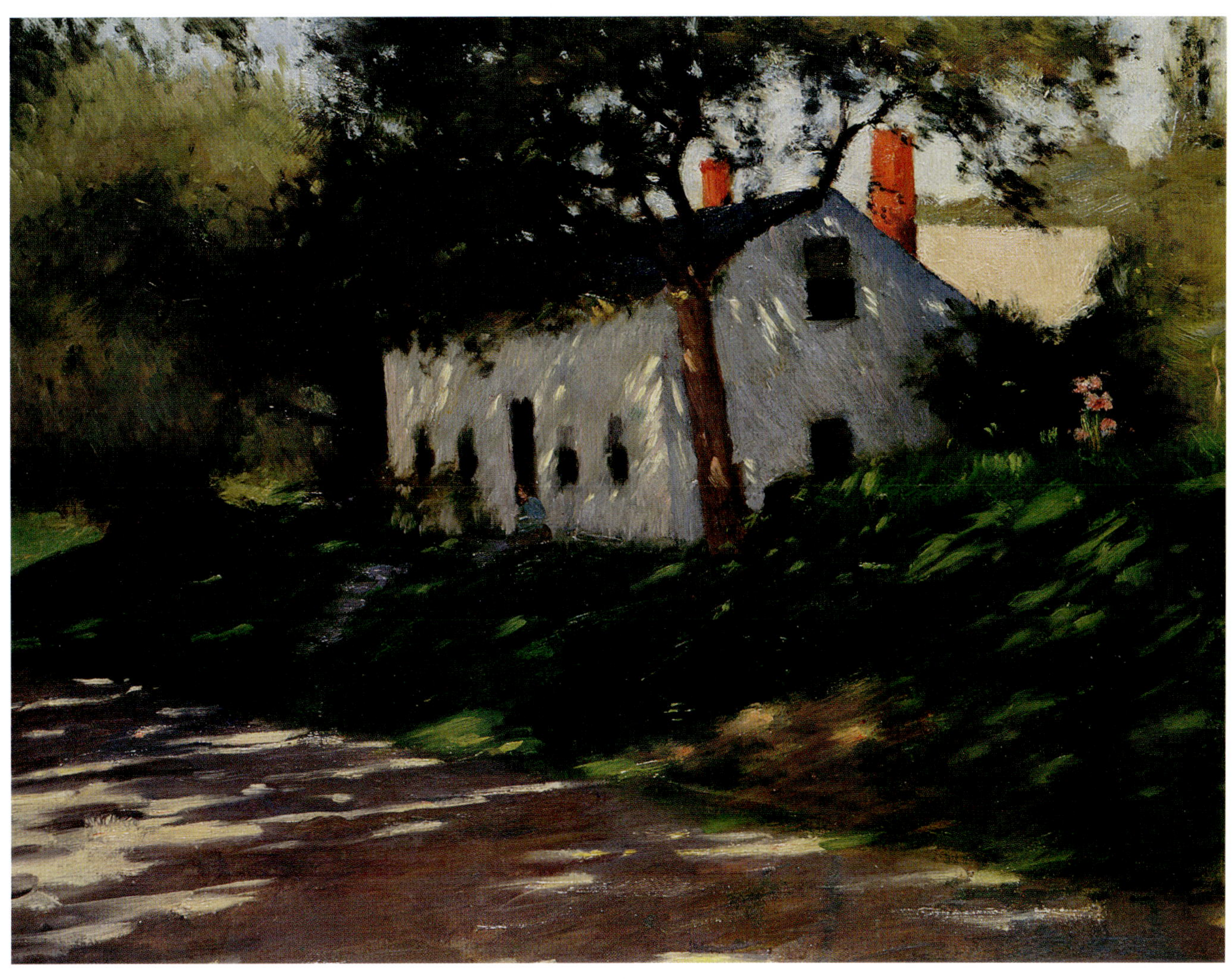

1

DENNIS BUNKER (1861–1890)

Roadside Cottage, Medfield, Mass., 1890

Oil on canvas, 17½ × 23½"

ACM 78.10

Courtesy Art Complex Museum

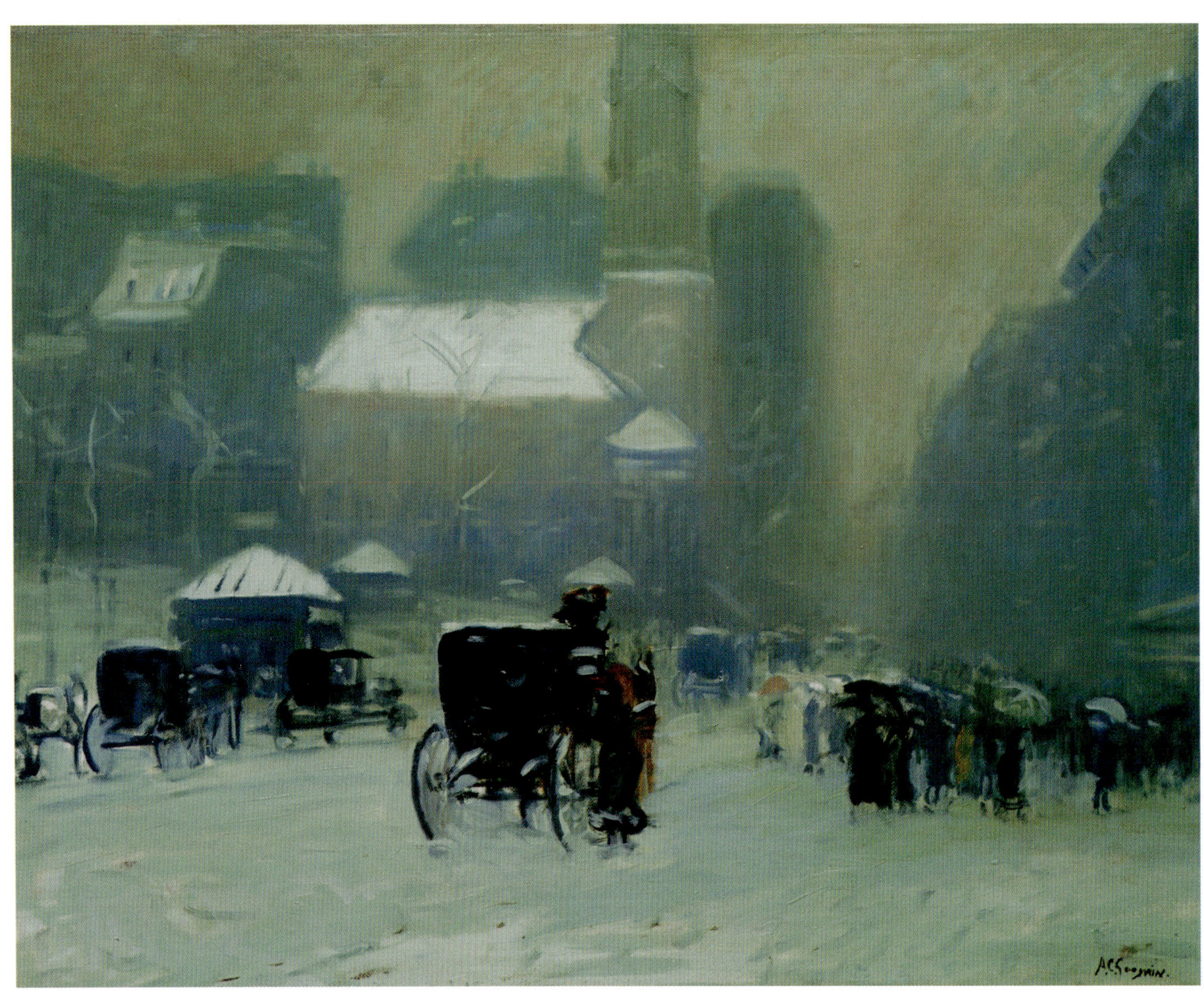

2

A. C. GOODWIN (1866–1929)

Snowy Day, Park Street Church, Boston, c. 1905–1910

Oil on canvas, 34 × 26¼"

ACM 80.330

Courtesy Art Complex Museum

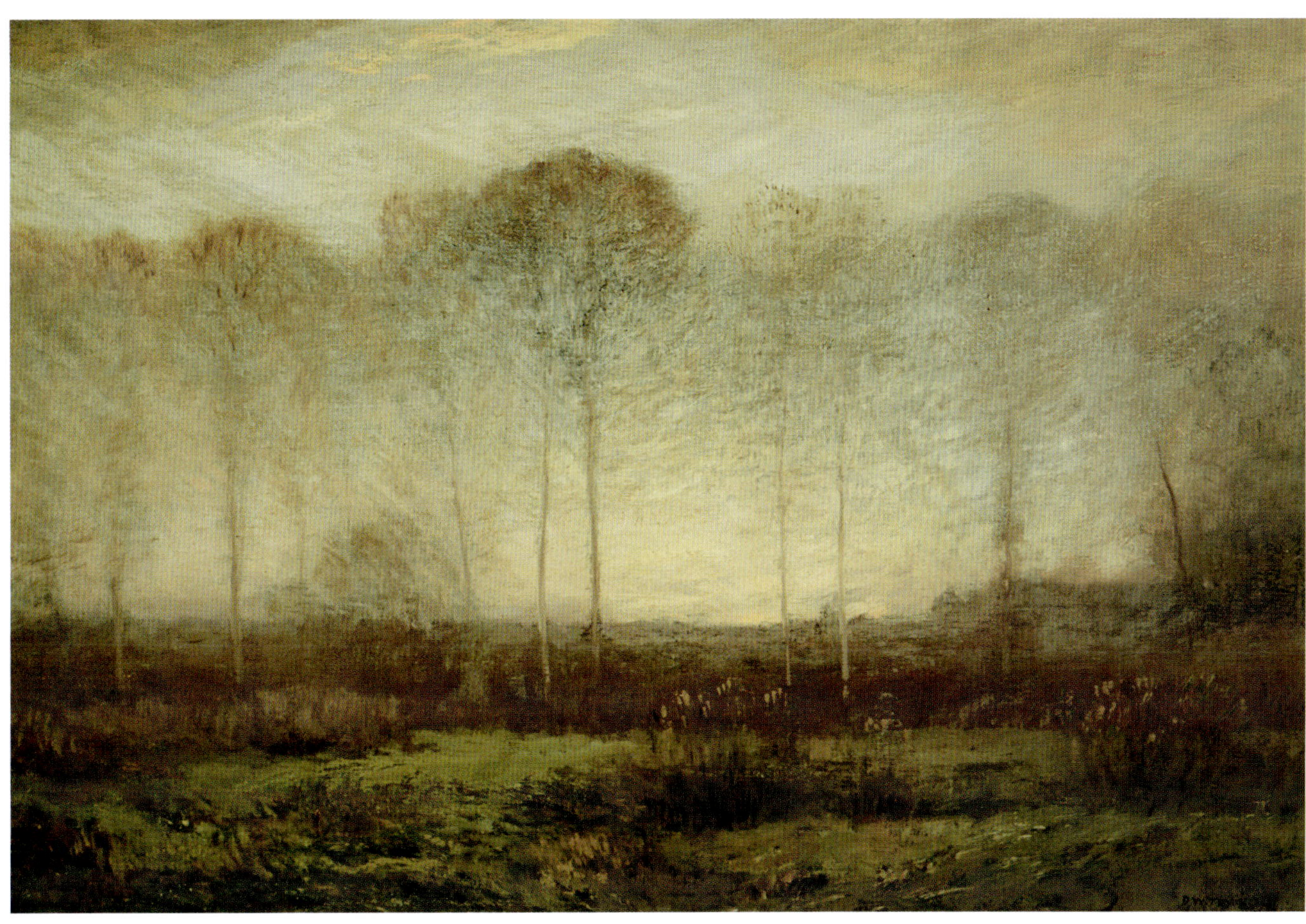

3
DWIGHT W. TRYON (1836–1925)
Dawn, 1906
Oil on canvas, 29½ × 19½"
ACM 80.334
Courtesy Art Complex Museum

focus, a series of astute connoisseurs and directors built a balanced collection of fine works in the areas of colonial portraiture, the Hudson River School, American Impressionism, the Ashcan School, the American Scene, and American Modenism (see figure 6).

The elegant nineteenth-century buildings that were so charitably bequeathed as museums by dutiful daughters in memory of their fathers, or designed by renowned architects, have required untold maintenance, repair, renovation, and expansion. Many have been transformed over the years into functional, climate-controlled, handsome exhibition galleries. The Lyman Allyn Art Museum in New London, Connecticut, opened in 1932 in a neoclassical-style building designed by Charles A. Platt. Three substantial additions and a major renovation ensued in the course of the next fifty years. The Newport

Art Museum and Art Association bought the historic John N. A. Griswold House, the premier example of the American Stick style architecture, designed by Richard Morris Hunt, to house classes and exhibitions in 1915 (see figures 7, 8). Shortly thereafter a group of citizens led by Gertrude Vanderbilt Whitney constructed a second building, a gallery dedicated to the memory of artist Howard Gardiner Cushing, who had died in 1916 (see figure 9). The Cushing Gallery was expanded and climate-controlled in 1991, and the ailing Griswold House is currently in the midst of a multimillion-dollar renovation. The Farnsworth Art Museum, in Rockland, Maine, while basically maintaining its original mission to focus on the art of Maine, has "physically reinvented itself" by renovation, as well as adding new wings and buildings. While the Farnsworth's original benefactor, Lucy Farnsworth, left a fund to create a library and gallery in memory of her father, she could hardly have imagined what the museum was to become: a monument to Maine's magnificent artistic legacy and a vital center for educational outreach in the state (see figures 10, 11). The Cape Museum of Fine Arts, founded in 1981 to "illustrate the role that Cape Cod and the Islands have played in American art," has also transformed its building into a state-of-the-art facility.

The dawn of the twenty-first century has thrown new light on these late-nineteenth- and twentieth-century institutions. In many cases, communities have changed. The gentrified, culturally elite patrons of yesteryear are waning. Demographics indicate that potential audiences will be increasingly diverse; at the same time competition for their time will be stiff. New England's community museums are rising to the challenge. The Fuller Museum of Art, in Brockton, Massachusetts, was founded in 1969 by the bequest of Myron L. Fuller, an entrepreneur and geologist. Brockton, in recent years an economically depressed area, is not a destination for Boston-area museum visitors. Operating presently as a regional museum, the Fuller has decided to refocus on contemporary craft, thus making it the only craft museum in New England. The Danforth Museum

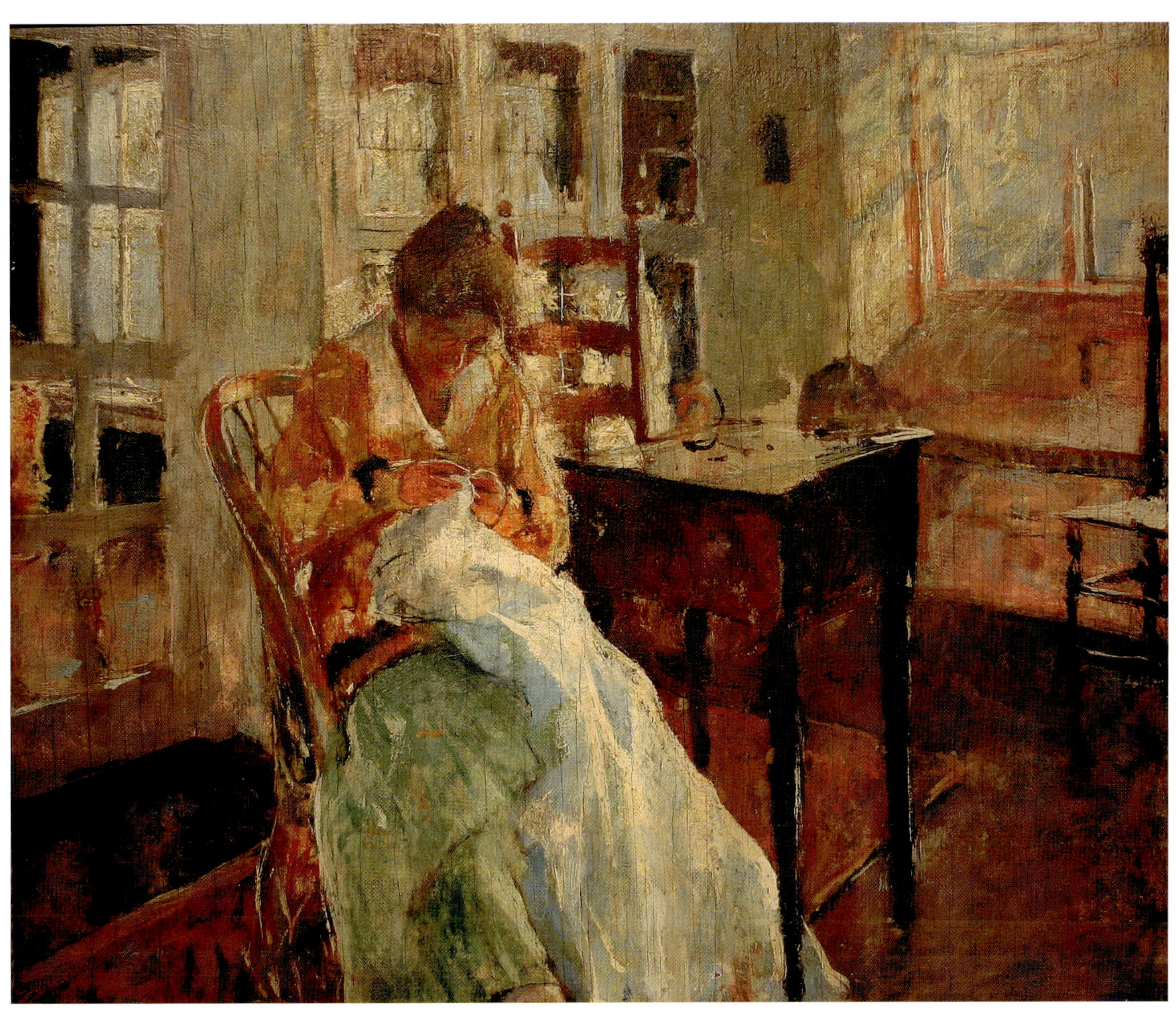

4

CHARLES WEBSTER HAWTHORNE (1872–1930)

The Dress Maker, 1915

Oil on panel, 25 × 30"

Collection of the New Britain Museum of American Art

Gift of Olga H. Knoepke

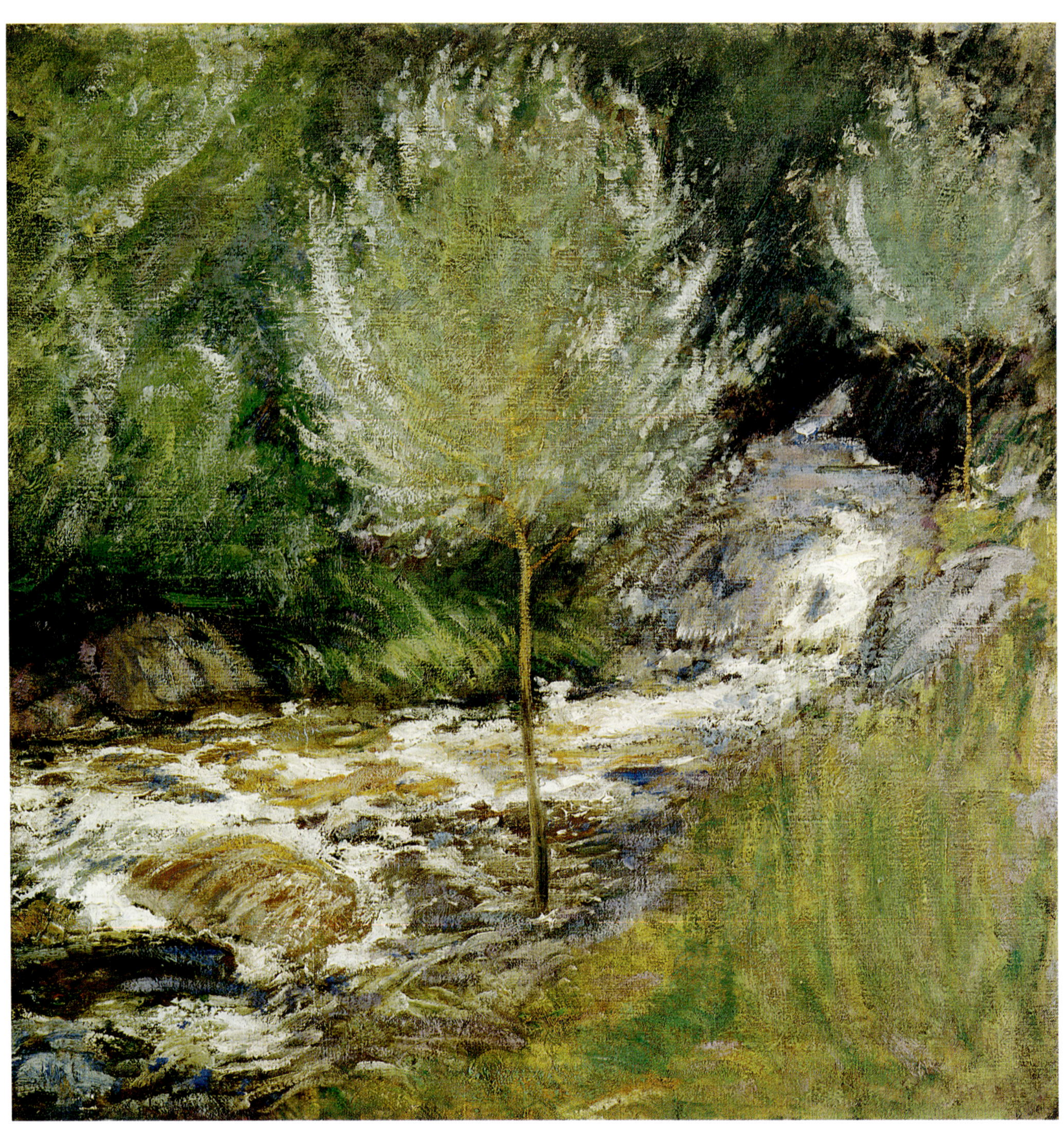

5

JOHN HENRY TWACHTMAN (1853–1902)

Horseneck Falls, Greenwich, c. 1890

Oil on canvas, 25¼ × 25¼"

Florence Griswold Museum

Gift of The Hartford Steam Boiler Inspection and Insurance Company

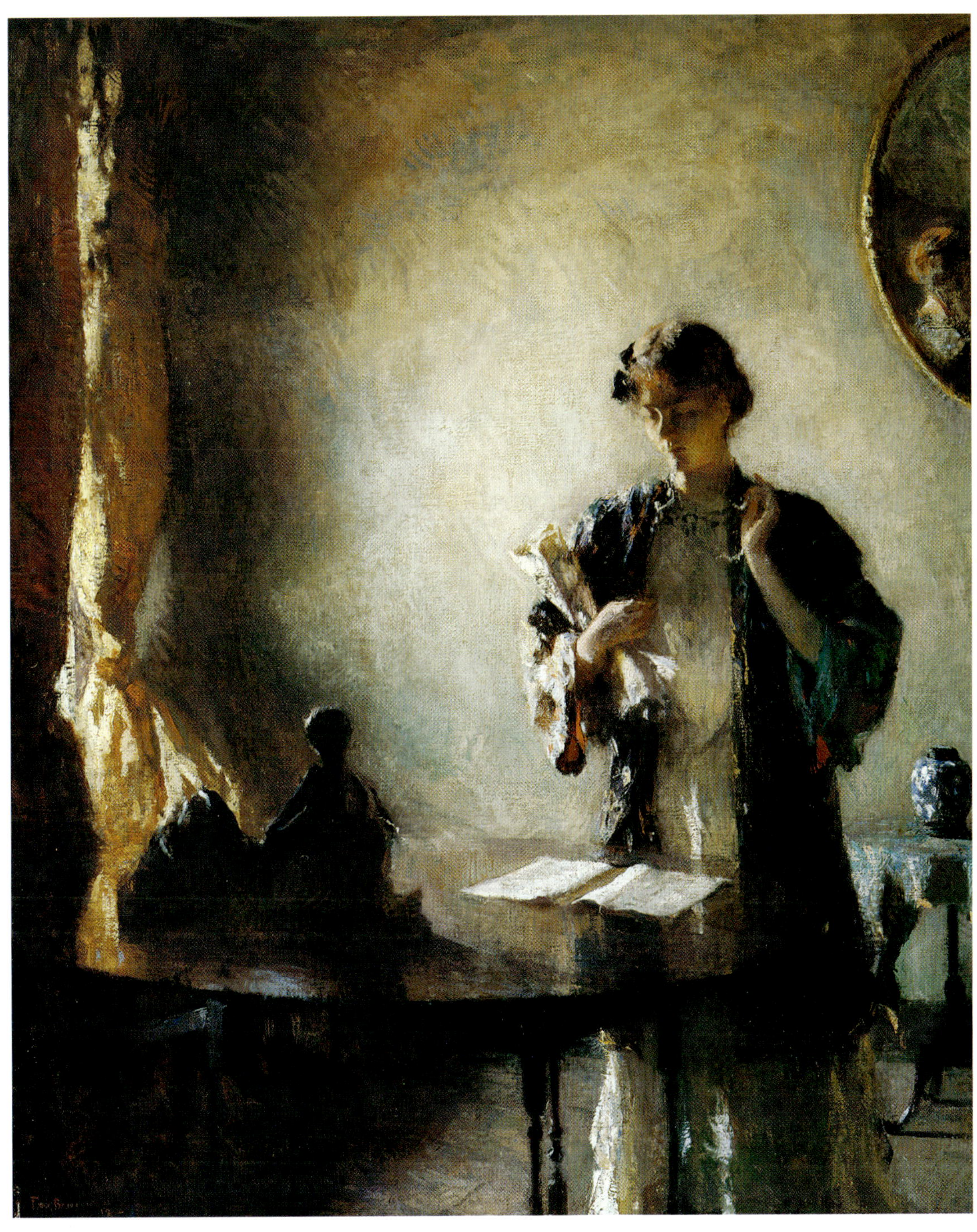

6

FRANK WESTON BENSON (1862–1951)

Figure in a Room (In the Study), 1912

Oil on canvas, 30 × 25"

Collection of the New Britain Museum of American Art

Alix W. Stanley Fund

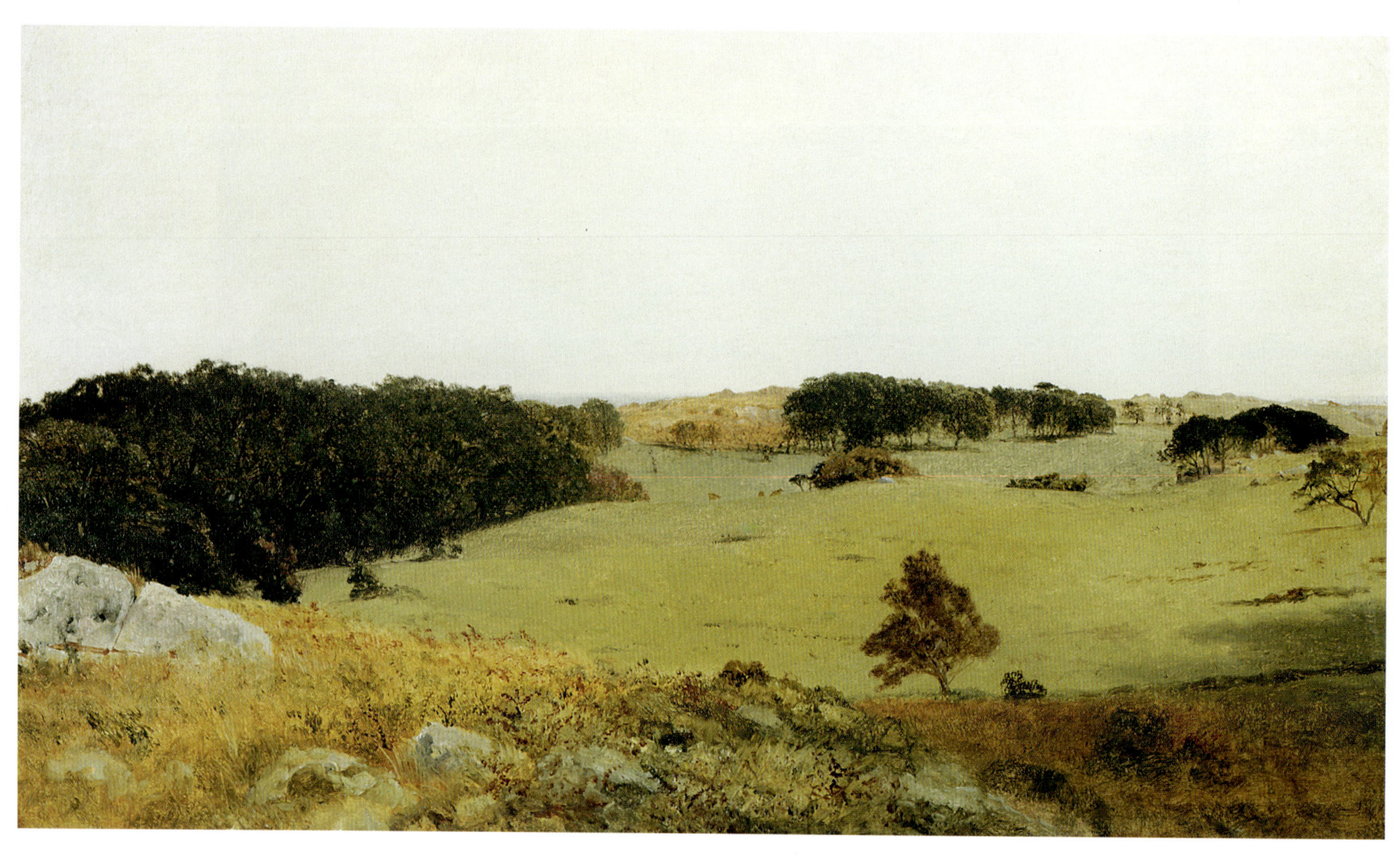

7

JOHN FREDERICK KENSETT (1816–1872)

Newport, c. 1870

Oil on canvas, 14 × 24¾"

Collection of the Newport Art Museum and Art Association

Gift of Mr. and Mrs. William Varieka

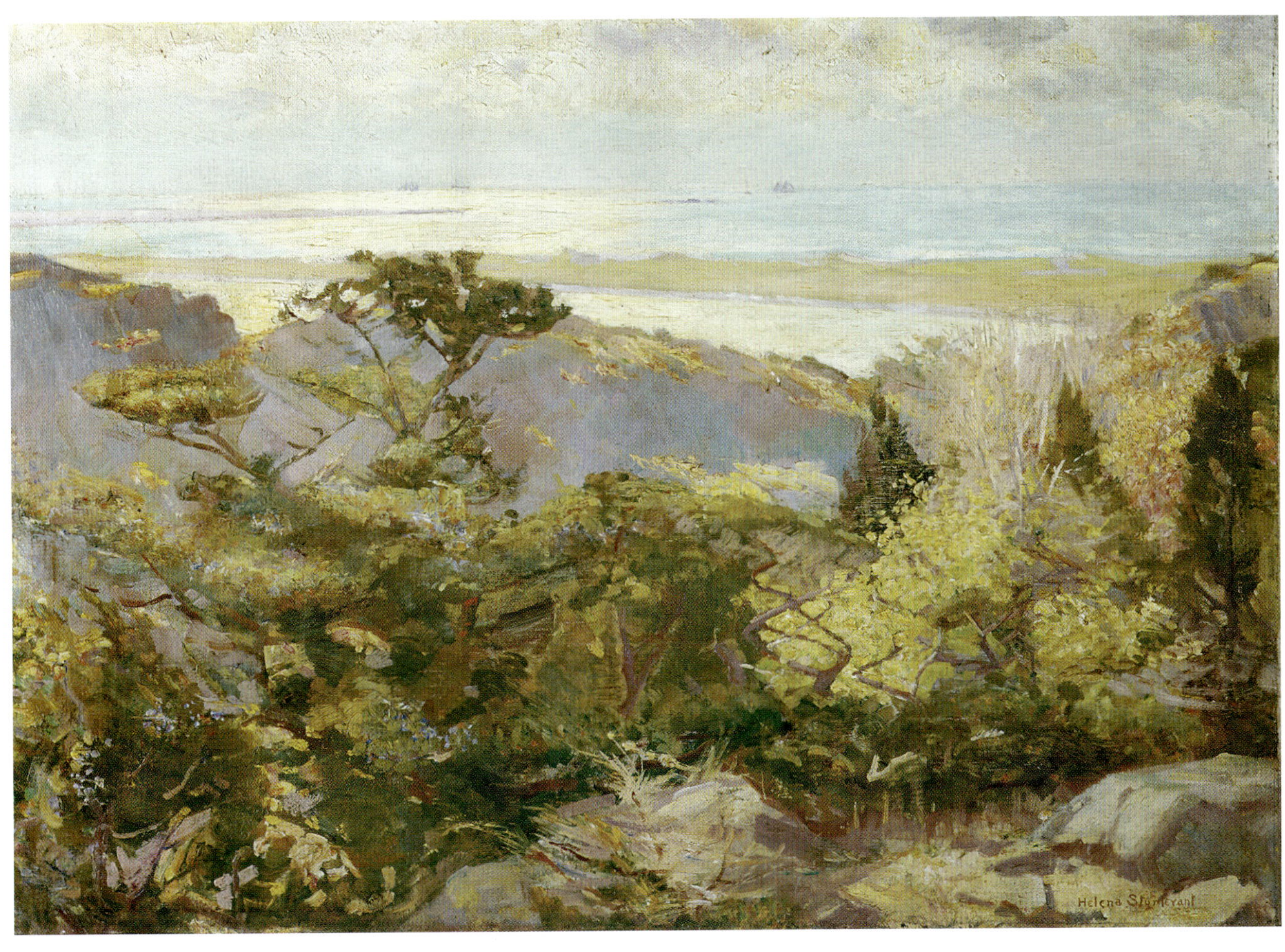

8

HELENA STURTEVANT (1872–1946)

Up on the Ridges of the Paradise Hills, 1925

Oil on canvas, 25 × 36"

Collection of the Newport Art Museum and Art Association

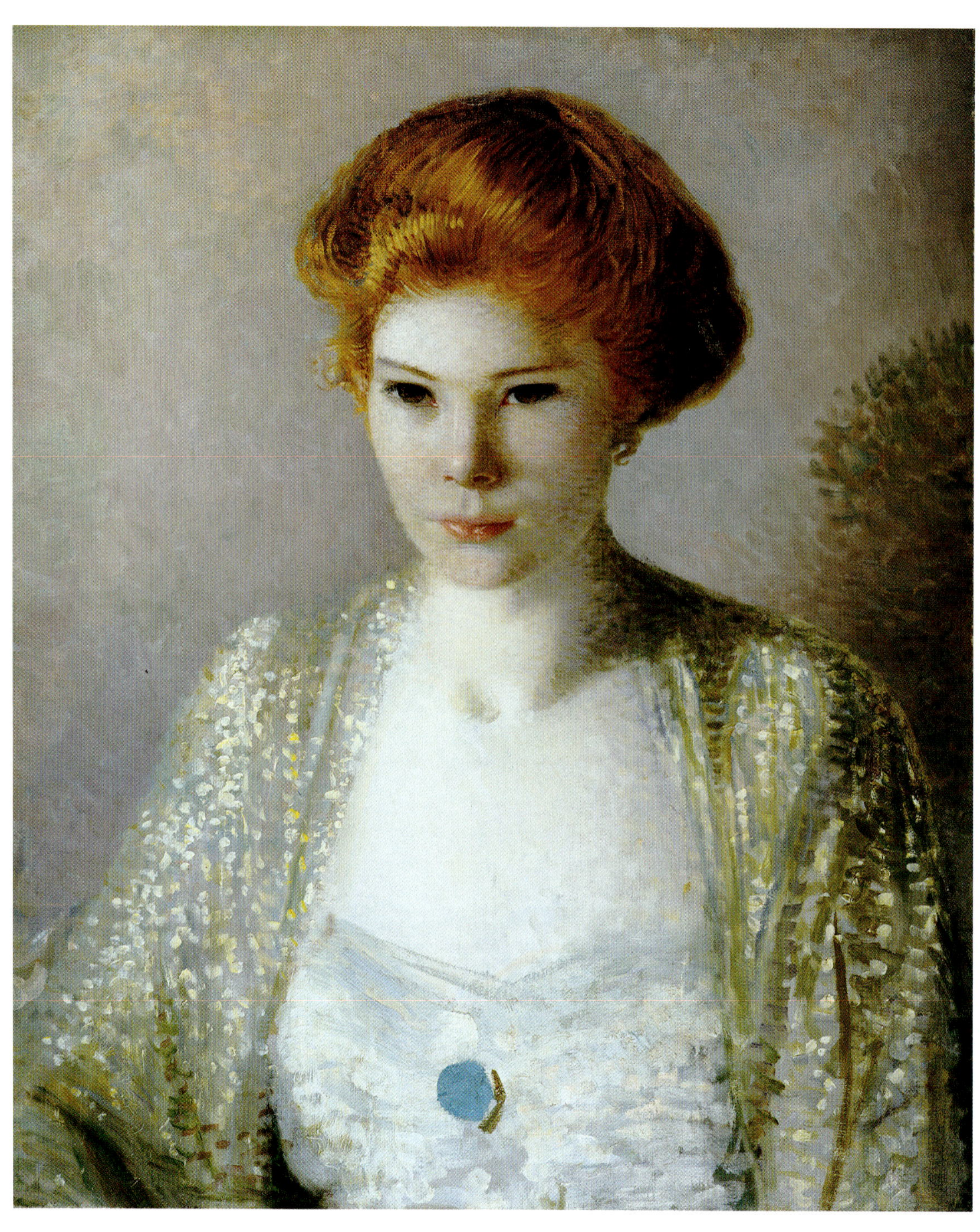

9

HOWARD GARDINER CUSHING (1869–1916)

Portrait of Ethel Cushing, c. 1904

Oil on canvas, 25½ x 21⅜"

Collection of the Newport Art Museum and Art Association

of Art has changed its mission to stress education in the visual arts and to define the area it serves—an increasingly multiethnic community west of Boston. The Fitchburg Art Museum, while maintaining founder Eleanor Norcross's goal to teach youth "the joy and inspiration of art," has collaborated with the public schools to create an arts magnet school, which is housed partly in the museum's galleries.

As part of the American Association of Museums' mandate to "place education—in the broadest sense of the word—at the center of their public service role," New England's community museums are consistently refocusing their missions and readdressing their constituencies.[2] Phrases such as "lively, compelling," "inspires and impacts," or "celebration and creation" now embellish the traditional missions of "collecting, preserving, exhibiting and interpreting" art. All the institutions do outreach to underserved audiences. In Maine, a rural state with great socioeconomic diversity, the Farnsworth has developed the Initiative for Maine Schools program, introducing students statewide to their artistic heritage. Museums are discovering that they can not only educate but also learn from their communities, as the tendency is to involve community members on boards and committees and to enlist their aid in programming and interpretation of exhibitions. Museum schools are finding that imaginative, hands-on activities are a successful way to engage large segments of the community—from small children to the elderly.

Nowhere is the connection between the past and the present more vital than at Fruitlands Museums in Harvard, Massachusetts. Founded by the scholar and collector Clara Endicott Sears as a home for her varied collections of Americana, including Shaker artifacts, Native American objects, American paintings, and items related to transcendentalist history, the 210-acre site has tremendous implications for learning from our cultural landscape (see figures 12, 13). Sears's vision was an educational one within the context of early-twentieth-century collecting and scholarship, and the previous mission adapted from her statements specified collecting, preserving, and

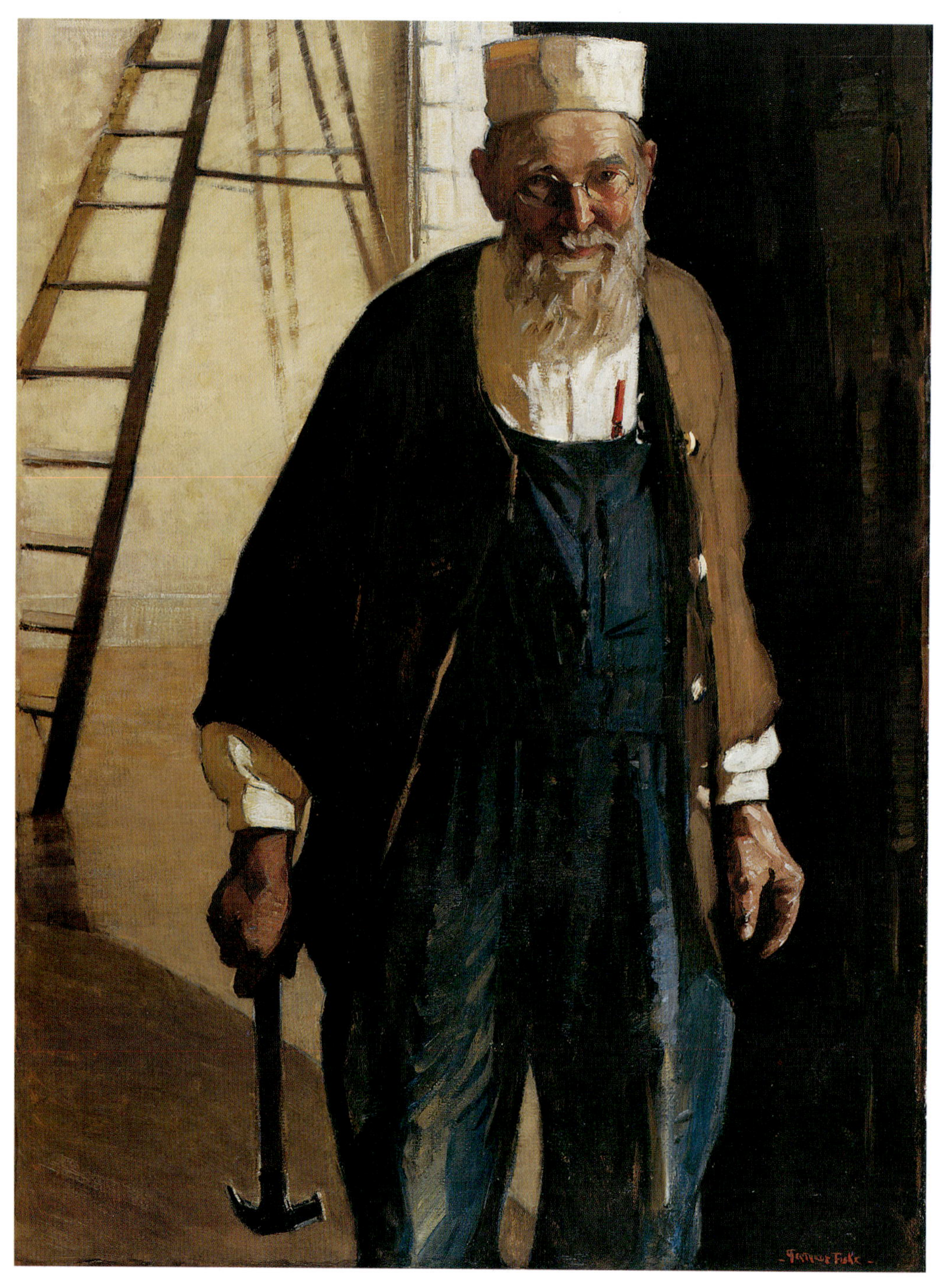

10

GERTRUDE HORSFORD FISKE (1878–1961)

The Carpenter, c. 1922

Oil on canvas, 54¼ × 40⅛"

Collection of the Farnsworth Art Museum

Gift of the Estate of Miss Gertrude Fiske, 1966

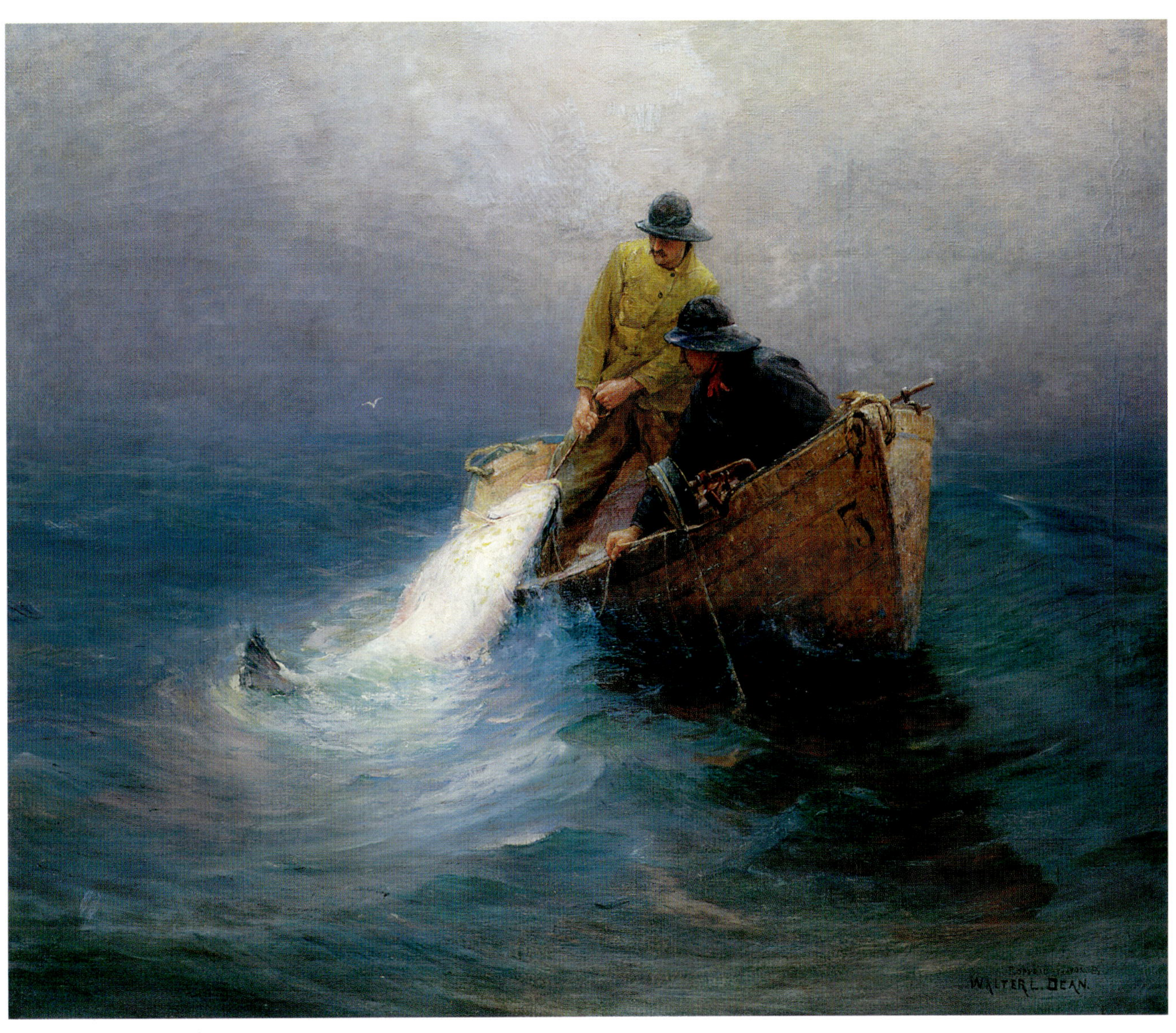

11

WALTER LOFTHOUSE DEAN (1854–1912)

On the Deep Sea, 1901

Oil on canvas, 40⅛ × 47¼"

Collection of the Farnsworth Art Museum

Gift of Mr. and Mrs. John Hill, Boston, 1971

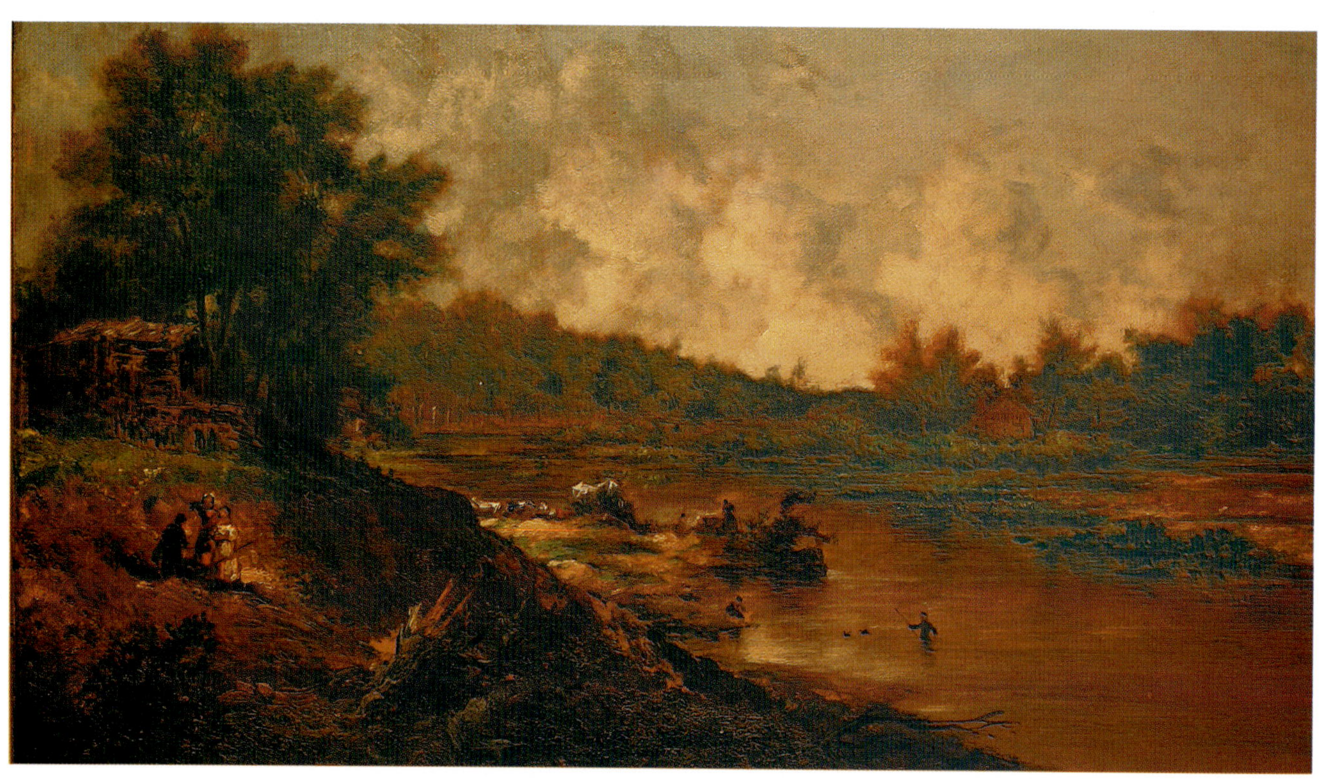

interpreting, "especially relating to the spiritual thought." After months of strategic planning and attempts to "capture the blending of Miss Sears's vision with our twenty-first century challenge," the staff and board of Fruitlands arrived at a new mission: "Fruitlands reveals the spirit and history of New England people and their relationship to the land." As New England's community art museums are energized and revitalized, we need to recognize the value of change and new direction. But just as important is the obligation to savor the accomplishments and foresight of those who have brought us this far.

12
GEORGE LORING BROWN (1814–1889)
On the River at Olneyville, R.I., 1863
Oil on artist board, 10⅜ x 18½"
Courtesy of Fruitlands Museums

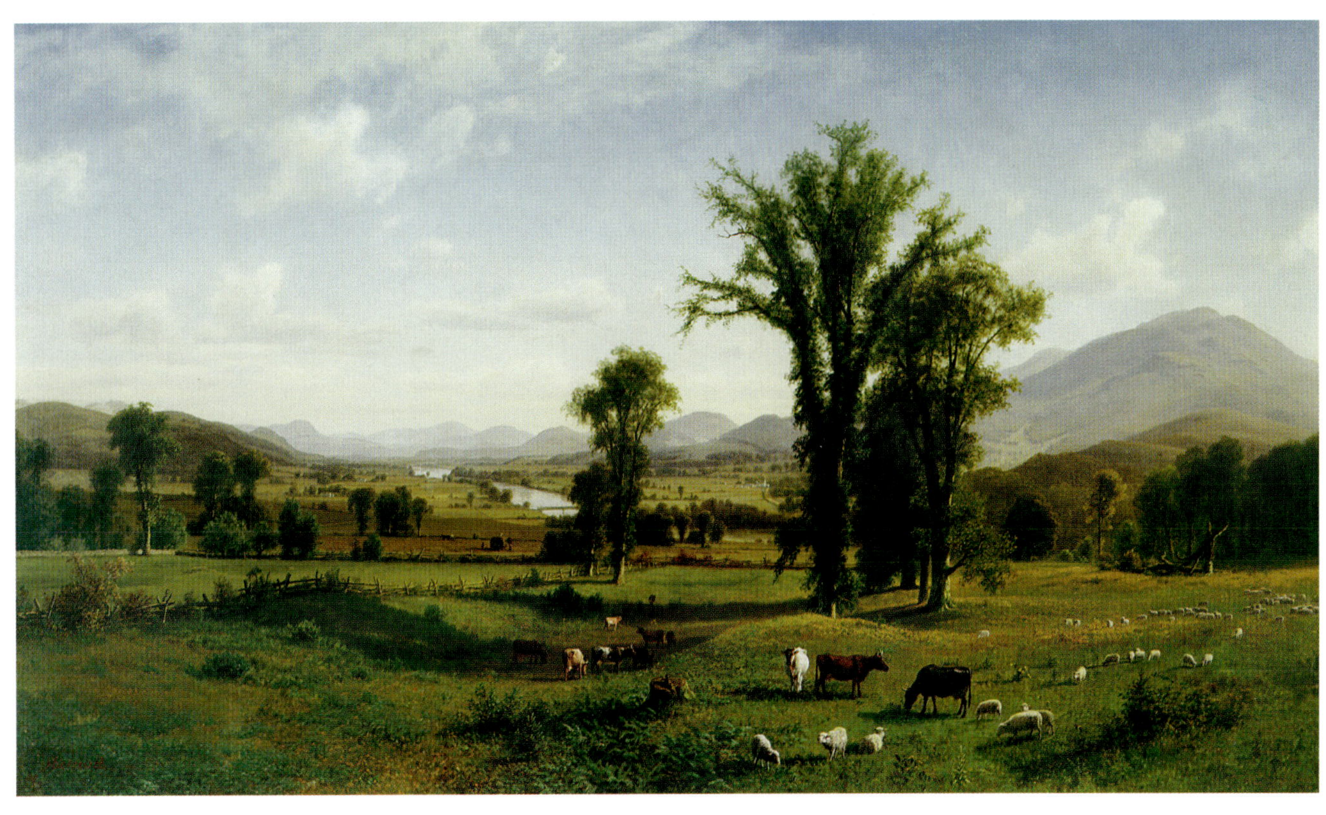

13

ALBERT BIERSTADT (1830–1902)

Mount Ascutney from Claremont, New Hampshire, 1862

Oil on Canvas, 31¼ × 47¼"

Courtesy of Fruitlands Museums

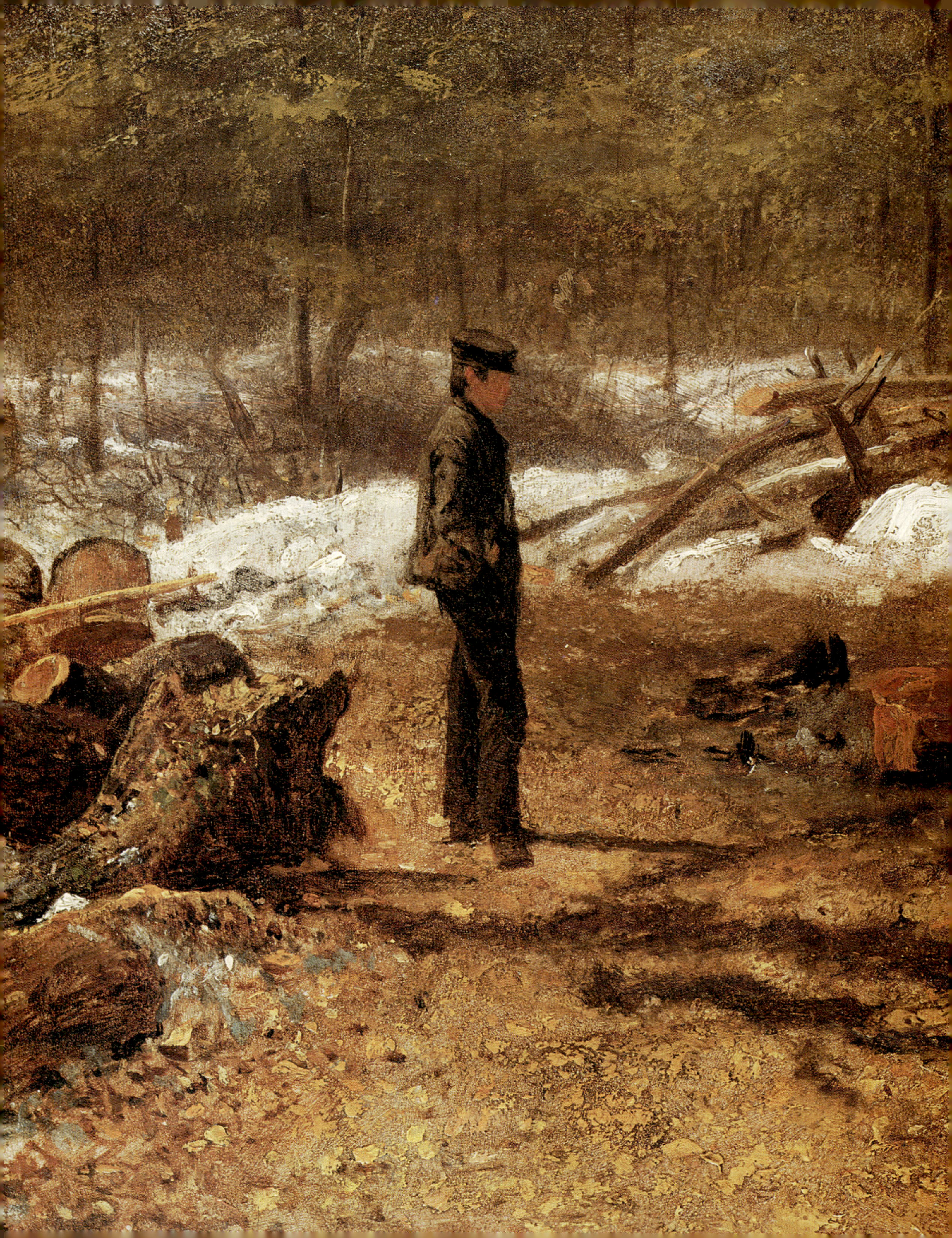

The American Artist in New England

Jack Becker

Director, Cheekwood Museum of Art

❦ AMERICAN ARTISTS HAVE found inspiration in the landscape, villages, cities, and ways of life in New England since the colonial era. This region has been the home to scores of artists whose professional lives revolved around the multitude of subjects they discovered there. The collections of the Consortium of New England Community Art Museums reflect that fascination, and this essay explores the appeal that this region had for American artists from 1850 to 1950. Over the course of this one-hundred-year period, artists drew their inspiration from the area's diverse landscape of mountains, valleys, salt marshes, and harbors. Others produced portraits or genre scenes reflecting the lives of the region's inhabitants. Yet, despite particular style or subject—portrayals of the seafaring coastline, the dramatic splendor of the White Mountains, or "ancient" colonial homes—when seen together, these images evoke a sense of place and way of life that for many is unmistakably New England.[1]

The Virtues of Rural Life

Without doubt the geography of New England seized the imagination of both artists and patrons alike throughout the nineteenth and twentieth centuries. Here artists discerned a landscape shaped by human endeavor yet still maintaining a natural beauty. Several of the earliest works are panoramic views of a harmonious and prosperous countryside. For example, Nelson Augustus Moore created an orderly landscape complete with a meandering country road, green meadows, and five distant church steeples that document the different

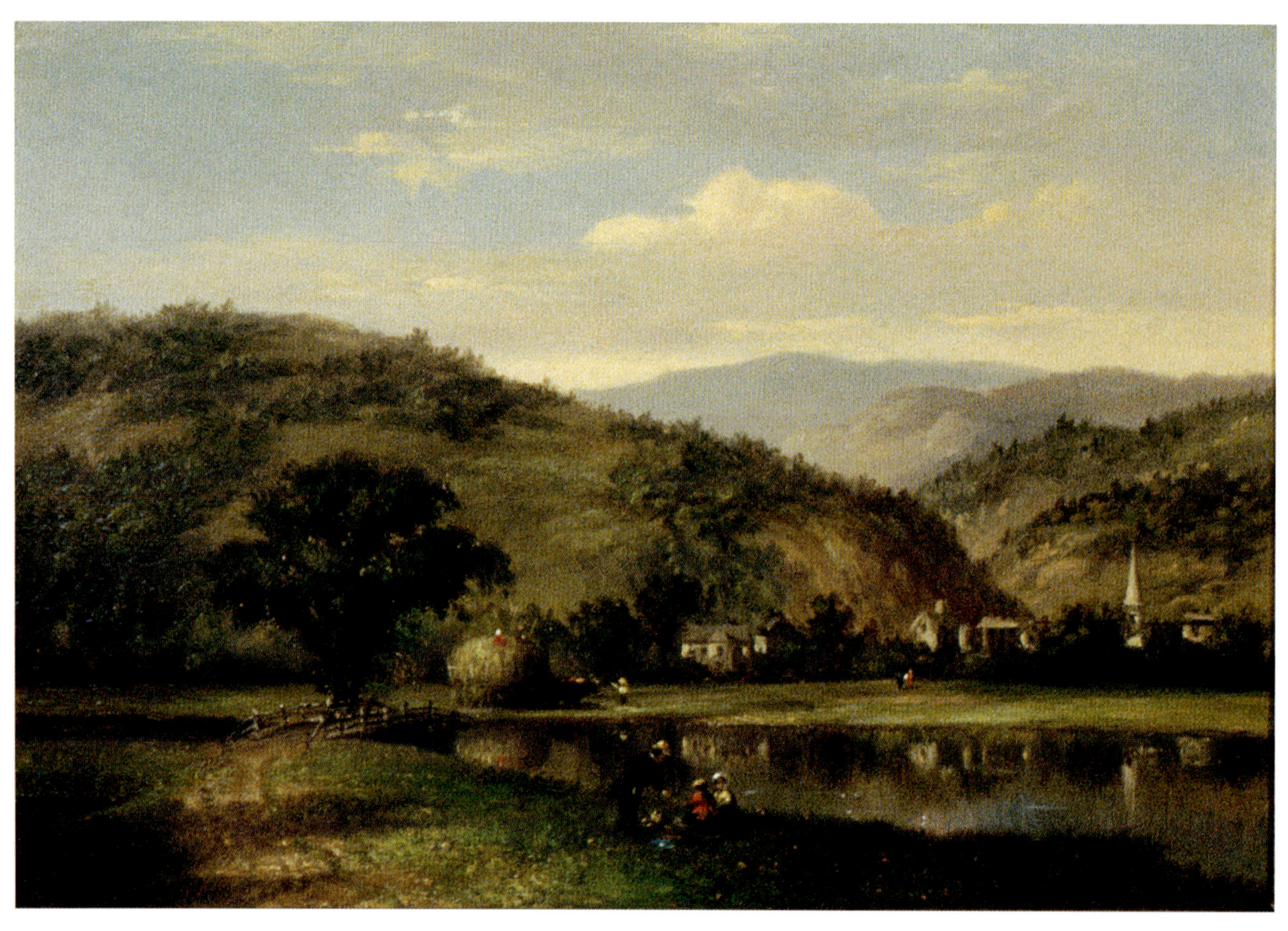

14

ROBERT DUNNING (1829–1905)

Stowe, Vermont, 1868

Oil on composition board, 6¼ × 9"

ACM 80.324

Courtesy Art Complex Museum

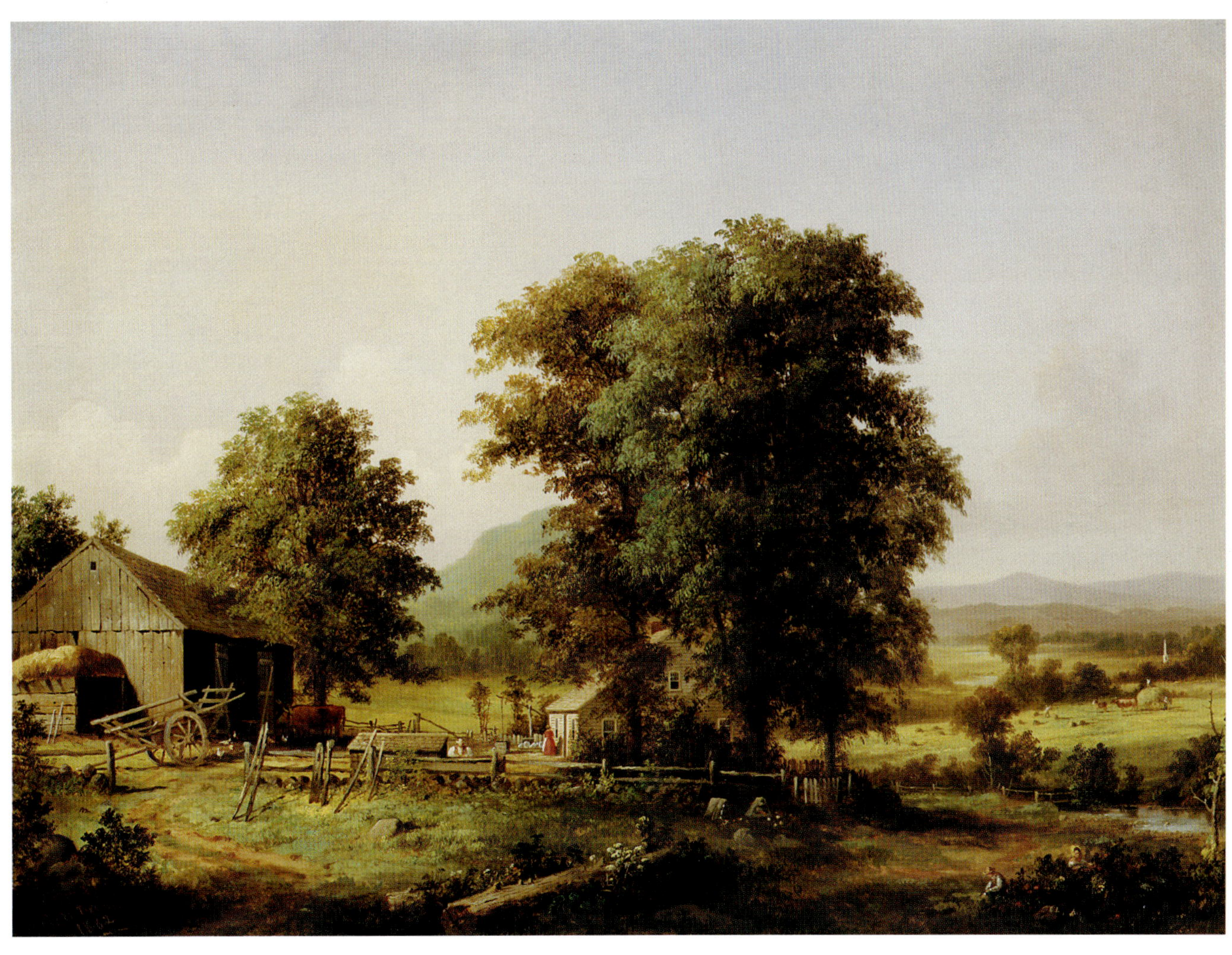

15

GEORGE HENRY DURRIE (1820–1863)

Summer Landscape, 1862

Oil on canvas, 22 × 30"

Florence Griswold Museum

Gift of The Hartford Steam Boiler Inspection and Insurance Company

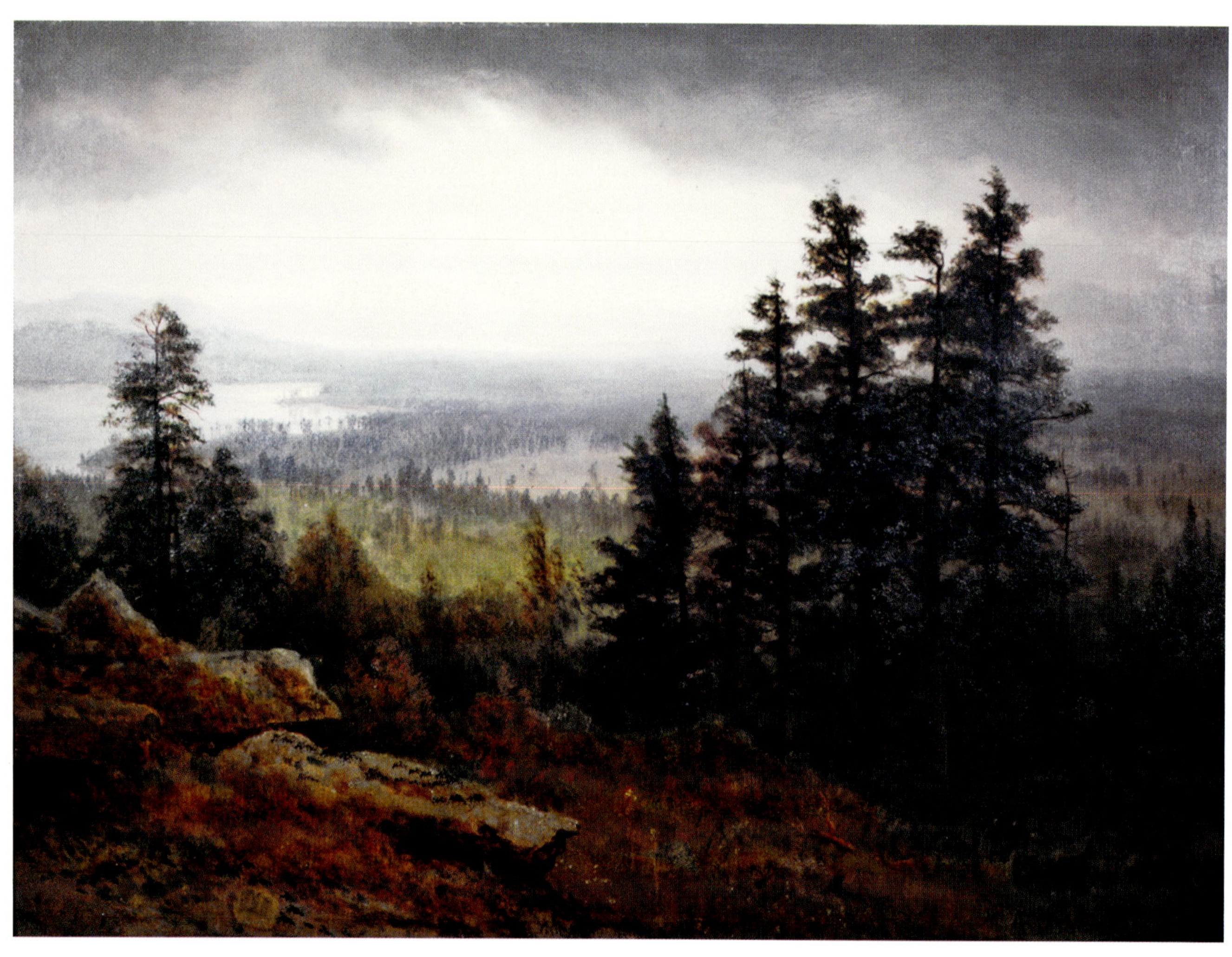

16

ALBERT BIERSTADT (1830–1902)

Near North Conway, New Hampshire, c. 1860–1862

Oil on paper on canvas, 18¾ x 26"

Collection of the Danforth Museum of Art

Gift of the Waters Foundation, 1997.65

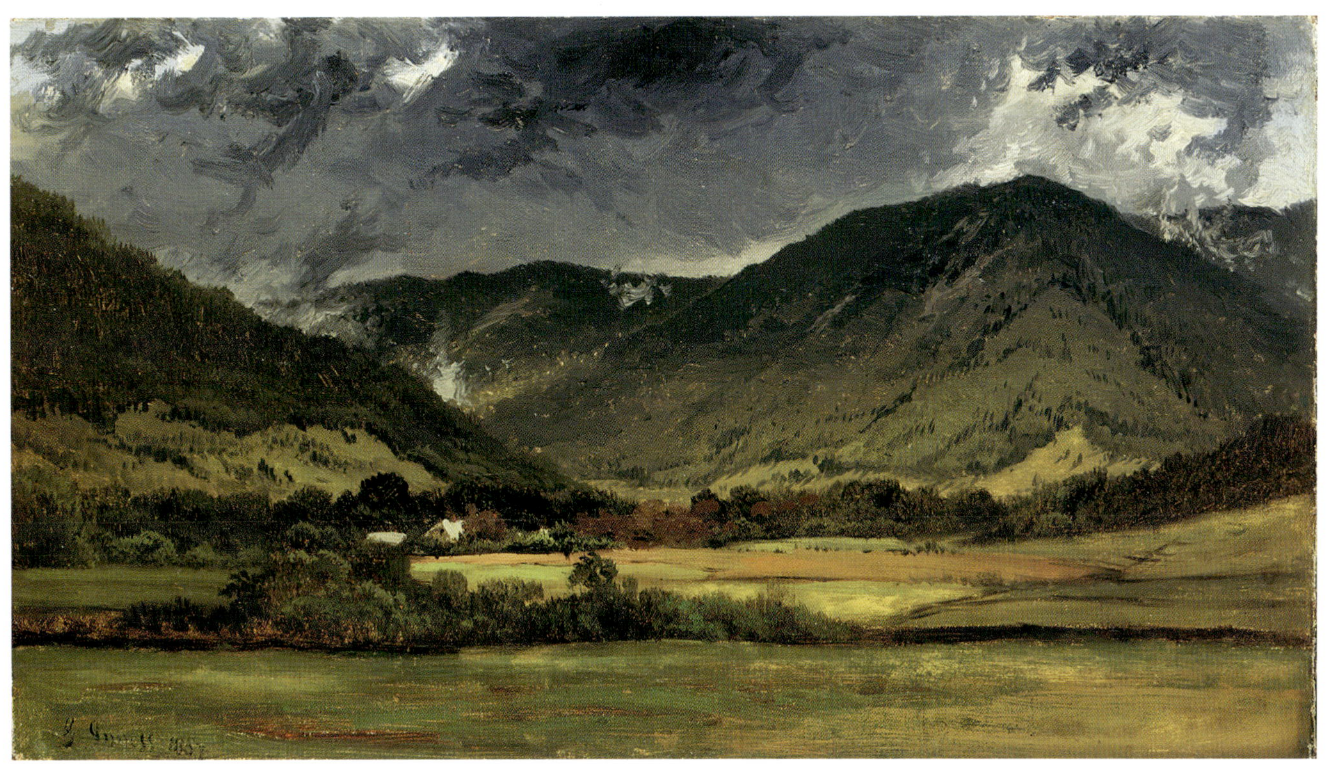

17
GEORGE INNESS (1825–1894)
In the White Mountains, Summer, 1859
Oil on canvas, 10⅛ × 18⅛"
Collection of the Farnsworth Art Museum
Museum purchase, 1944

faiths making their home in Waterbury, Connecticut (see figure 51). Robert Dunning celebrated the pastoral countryside of Stowe, Vermont, and George Henry Durrie created an idyllic image of the Connecticut landscape complete with shining sun, a prosperous homestead, a bountiful harvest, and a distant steeple (figures 14, 15). Other artists were entranced by one of the region's most dramatic subjects, the White Mountains, a theme that generations of painters turned to for inspiration. For example, working in a highly realistic manner, Albert Bierstadt, the painter of the American West, captured the White Mountains of North Conway, New Hampshire (figure 16).[2] His contemporary, George Inness, also painted the White Mountains but employed a more painterly approach with freer brushwork, brighter colors, and a more informal composition (figure 17).[3]

Some painters captured ways of life closely connected with the rural landscape of New England. Returning to his native Maine,

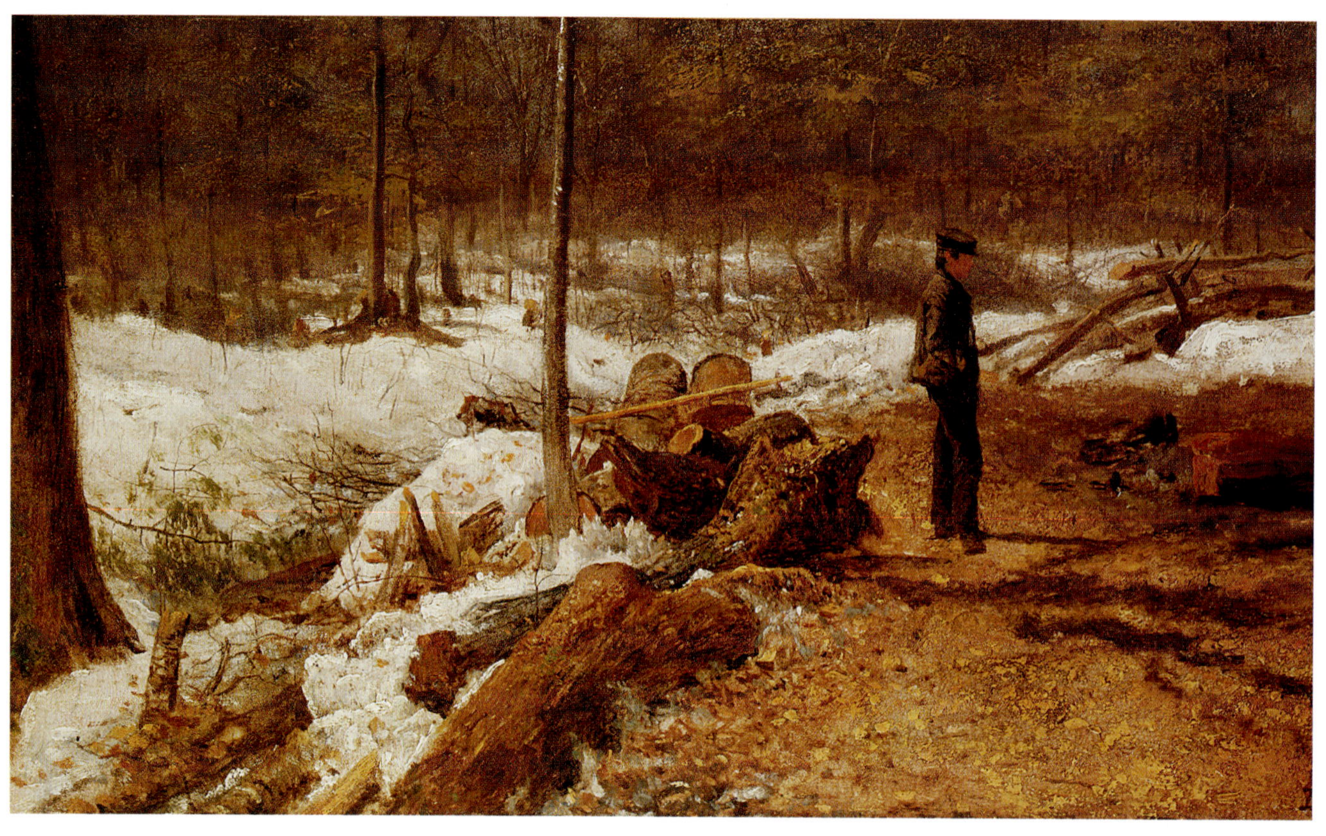

18

EASTMAN JOHNSON (1824–1906)
A Boy in the Maine Woods, c. 1868
Oil on canvas, 12 x 20⅛"
Collection of the Farnsworth Art Museum
Bequest of Mrs. Elizabeth B. Noyce, 1997

Eastman Johnson produced several images of maple sugaring as well as images of single woodcutters including *A Boy in the Maine Woods* (figure 18).[4] Another artist native to Maine, Harrison Brown, would earn acclaim for his mountain landscapes and his marine paintings. His highly detailed interior of a New England barn portrays the prosperity of this farm and includes a landscape view of the White Mountains through the open doors (figure 19).

Whereas some painters turned to the villages, mountains, and agricultural traditions of New England, others looked to the coast for its variety of subjects and broad interpretive range—from tranquil harbors to the high drama of rugged seas. An avid painter of coastal harbors, Fitz Hugh Lane, illustrated maritime activities in Maine during the middle of the nineteenth century (figures 20, 21). In his *Shipping in Down East Waters* a brigantine with a full cargo of

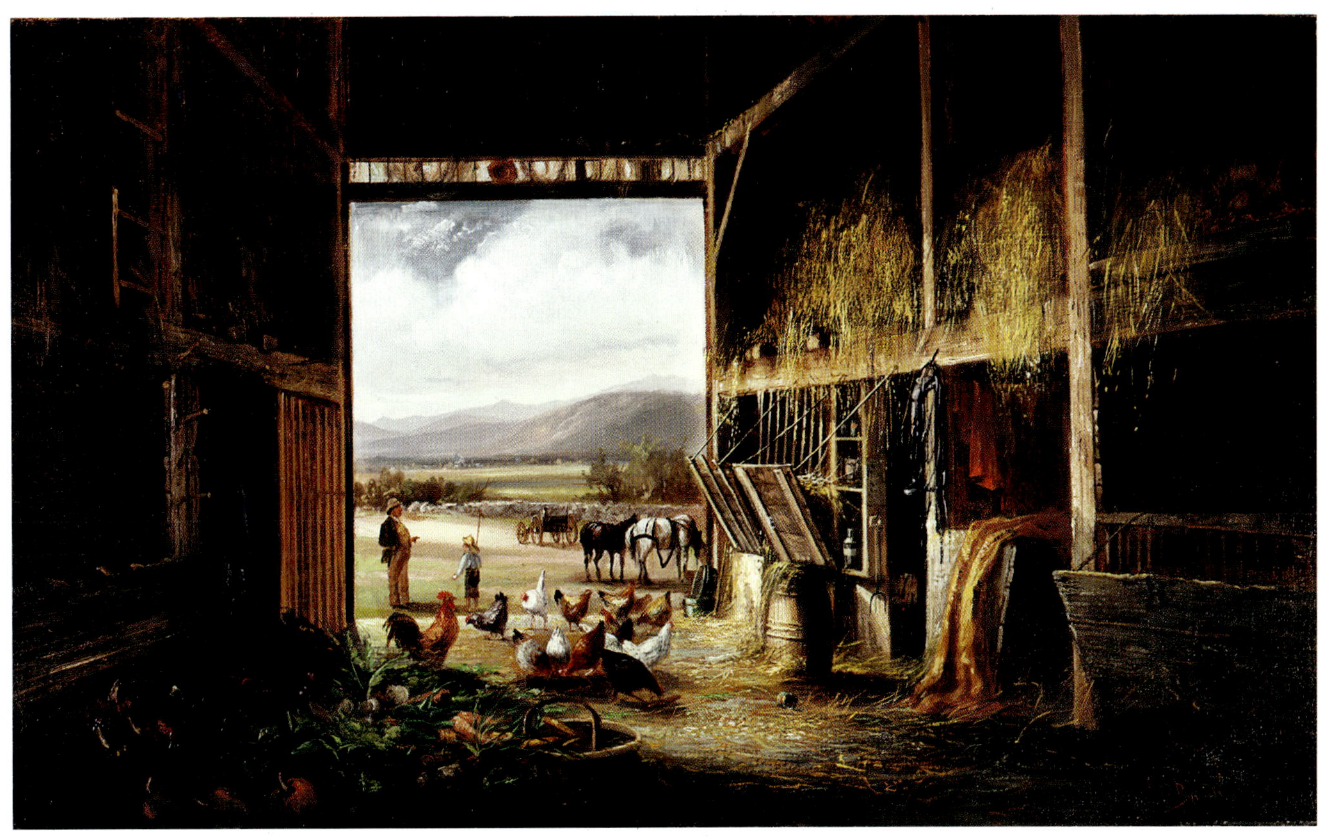

19
HARRISON BROWN (1831–1915)
Barn Interior, c. 1885
Oil on canvas, 17½ × 29"
Courtesy of Fruitlands Museums

lumber products occupies the center of the painting surrounded by other vessels, all depicted under a peaceful evening sky.[5] Contrasting Lane's illustration of the economic prosperity of coastal harbors, William Trost Richards found his niche creating luminous seascapes of muted tones, horizontal in format (figure 22).[6] Another painter, Martin Johnson Heade, was drawn to the coastal marshes of Massachusetts. In *Ipswich Marshes* (figure 23), Heade depicts a large expanse of open marsh, eloquently rendering the light, atmosphere, and weather effects of this coastal environment.[7] But for Heade, as for so many other artists of this era, the natural landscape showed signs of man's habitation, with grazing animals in the foreground and perfectly stacked haystacks dotting the marsh. For these artists, the New England landscape suggested a place where man lived in harmony with the natural beauty of the region.

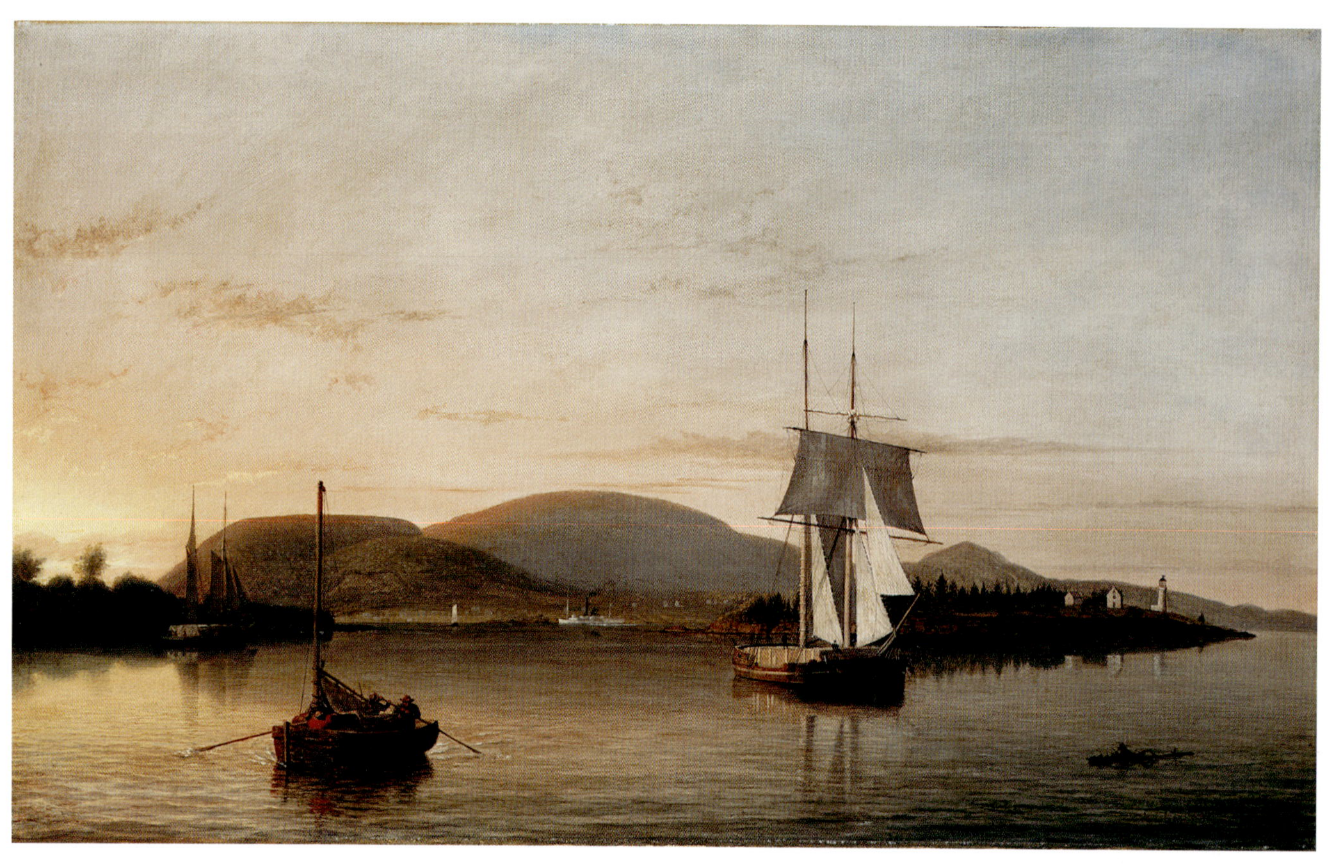

20

FITZ HUGH LANE (1804–1865)

Camden Mountains from the South Entrance to the Harbor, 1859

Oil on canvas, 22⅛ × 36¼"

Collection of the Farnsworth Art Museum

Bequest of Mrs. Elizabeth B. Noyce, 1997

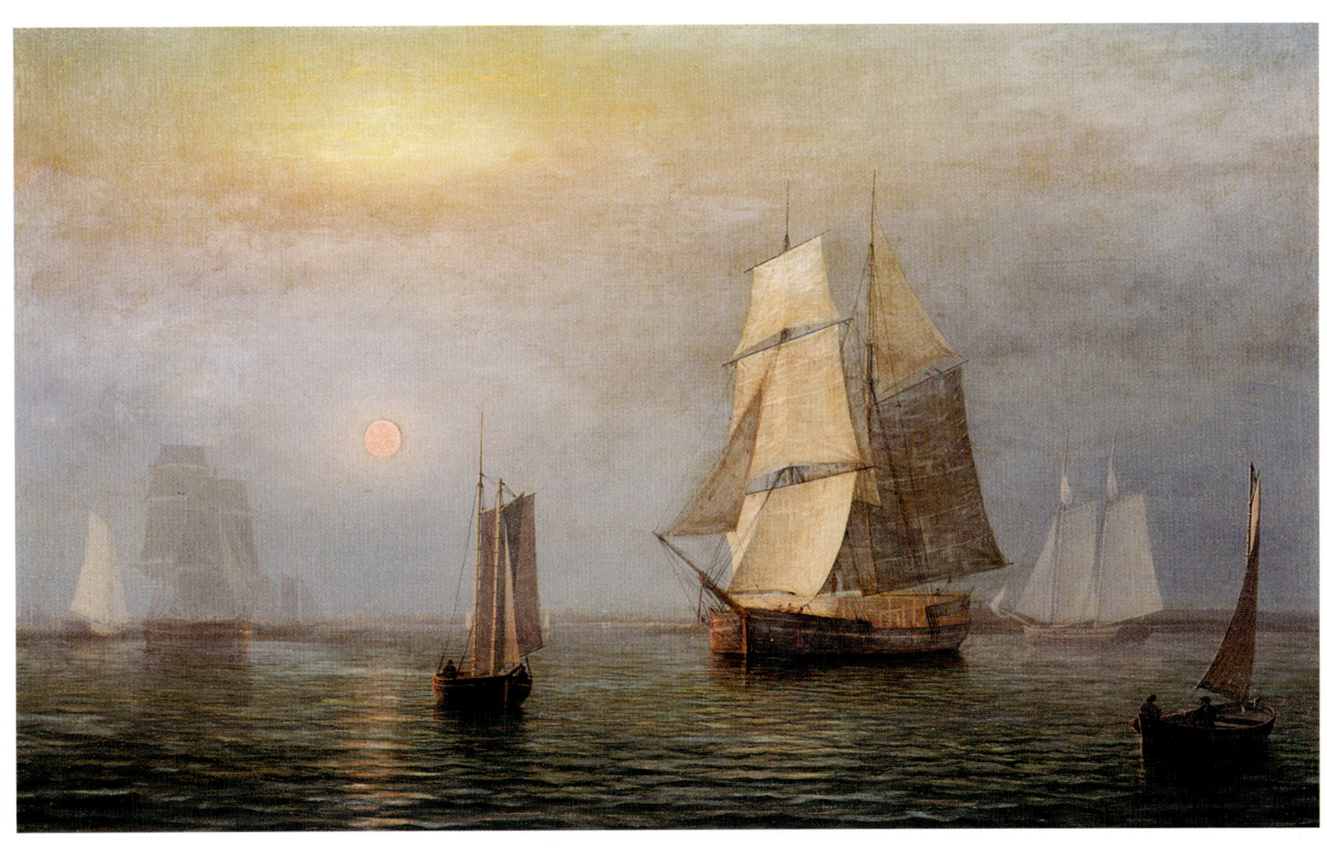

21

FITZ HUGH LANE (1804–1865)

Shipping in Down East Waters, 1854

Oil on canvas, 17¾ × 29¾"

Collection of the Farnsworth Art Museum

Museum purchase, 1960

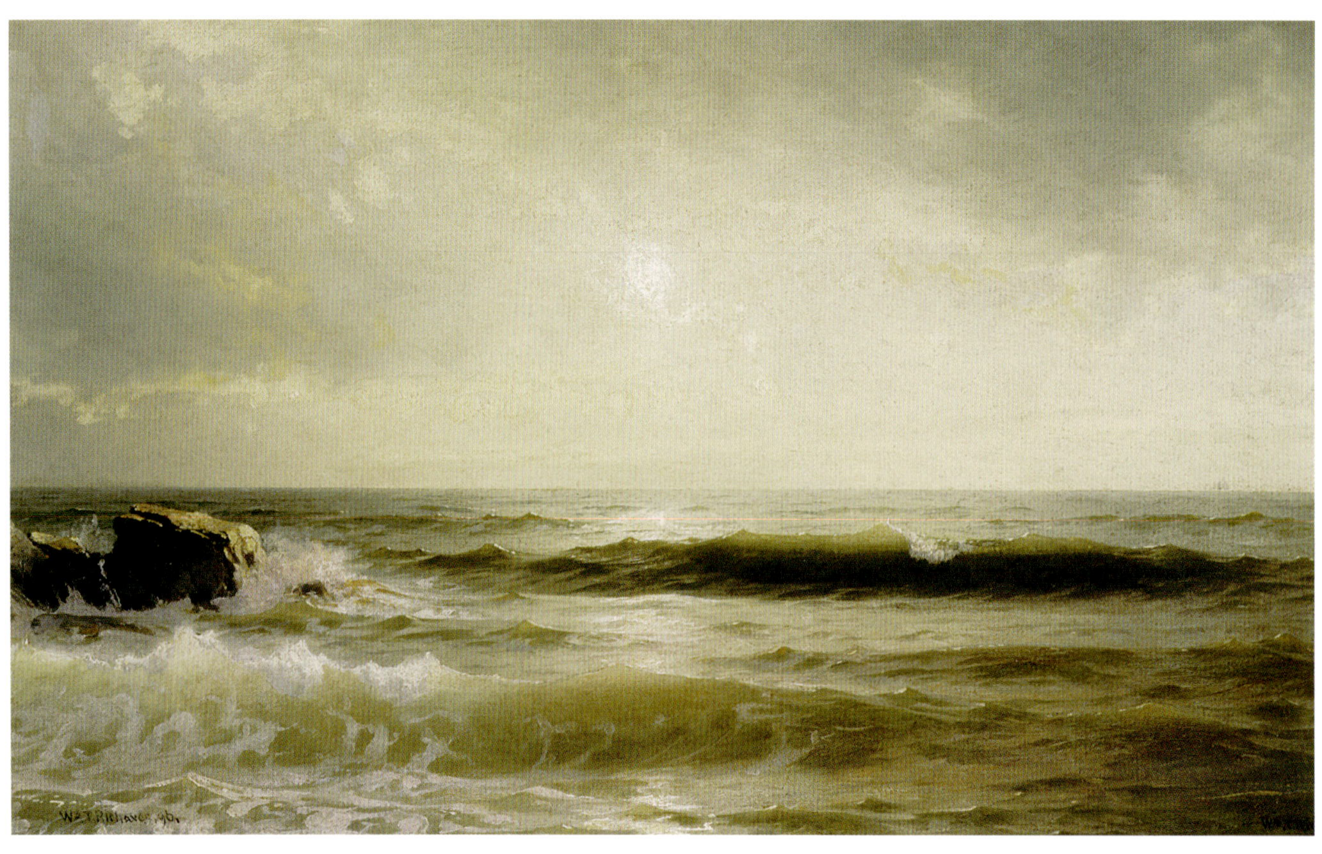

22

WILLIAM TROST RICHARDS (1833–1905)

Off the South Shore, 1896

Oil on canvas, 20¼ × 32¼"

Collection of the Newport Art Museum and Art Association

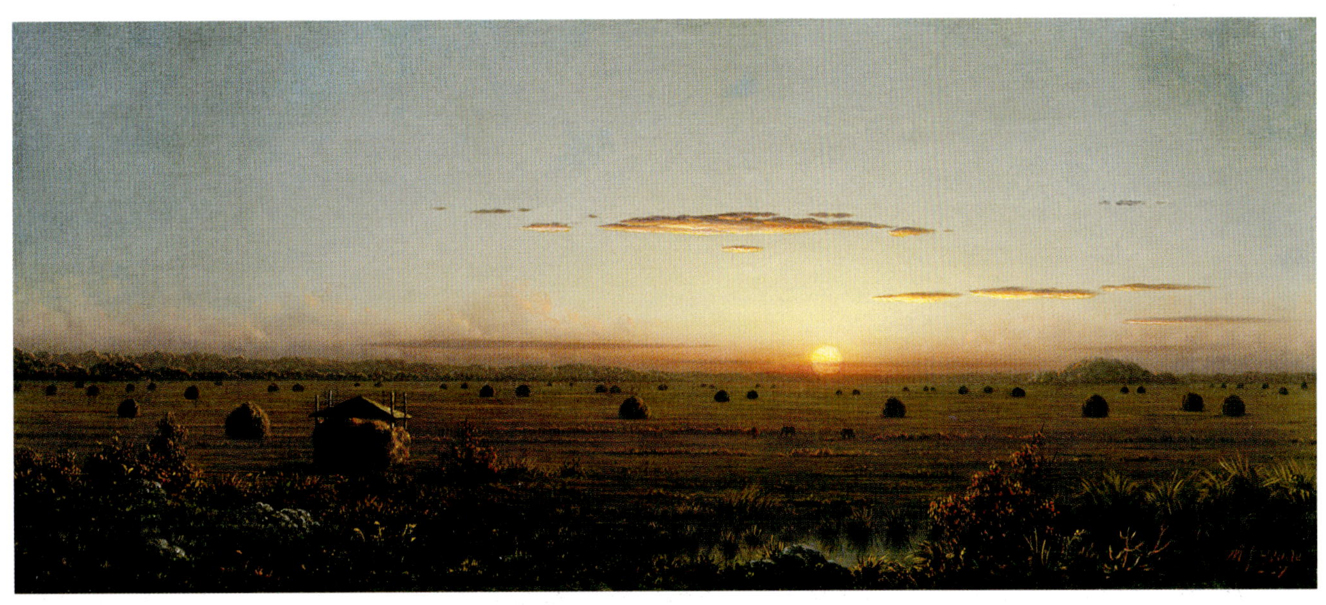

23

MARTIN JOHNSON HEADE (1819–1904)

Ipswich Marshes, 1867

Oil on canvas, 12 × 28"

Collection of the New Britain Museum of American Art

Stephen B. Lawrence Fund

Art Colonies in New England

Successive generations of artists were drawn to New England at the close of the nineteenth and beginning of the twentieth century. The noted American Impressionist Childe Hassam traveled throughout New England on several occasions in search of subject matter (figures 24, 25).[8] During this period, Hassam and other artists were members of the many art colonies that proliferated throughout New England. Painters discovered picturesque subjects, inexpensive lodgings, the camaraderie of other creative souls, and a respite from city life in the small villages of New England. Although each colony developed its own character, many of the artists who frequented a particular locale were drawn to its rural charm and historic character, producing images suggestive of these associations.[9]

Conveniently located near New York City, Connecticut became the home for many artists. One of the most famous artists to settle in the state, Julian Alden Weir, drew his inspiration from the Connecticut countryside, and today his farm and the landscape that inspired him are preserved as a national historic site (figure 26). Other artists from New York and elsewhere, including Henry Ward Ranger[10] and William Robinson, descended upon the colonial town of Old Lyme, Connecticut, where they formed an important colony of artists (figures 27, 28).[11] There, they discovered a landscape and village untouched by the industrial revolution. Further north the Massachusetts coastline was also the home of several art colonies. The painter Charles Webster Hawthorne, who had lifelong ties to the New England coast, was responsible for the development of an art colony in Provincetown on Cape Cod (see figure 4). He taught there for thirty years and drew his inspiration from the local landscape and people. Following in Hawthorne's lead, George Grosz, Arthur Diehl, Ross Moffett, and Lucy L'Engle enjoyed careers that revolved around the Cape Cod region (figures 29, 30, 31, 32). The historic fishing port of Gloucester, Massachusetts, also attracted painters from Boston and New York. One of the lesser-known artists, Walter Lofthouse Dean,

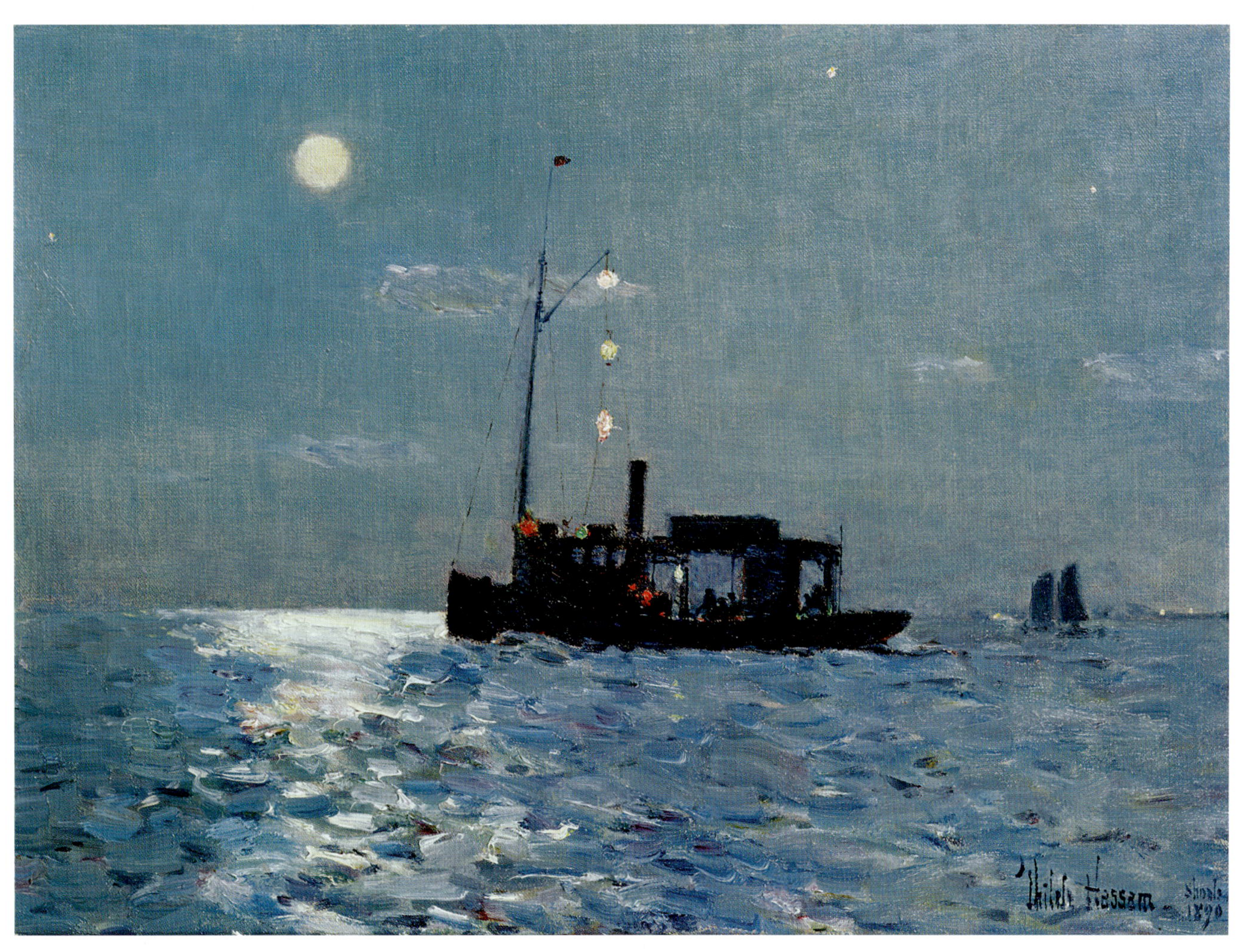

24

CHILDE HASSAM (1859–1935)

Isle of Shoals, Moonlight, 1890

Oil on canvas, 12¾ × 9½"

Collection of the Fitchburg Art Museum

Gift of Carl and Rosamund Pickhardt, 1994.4

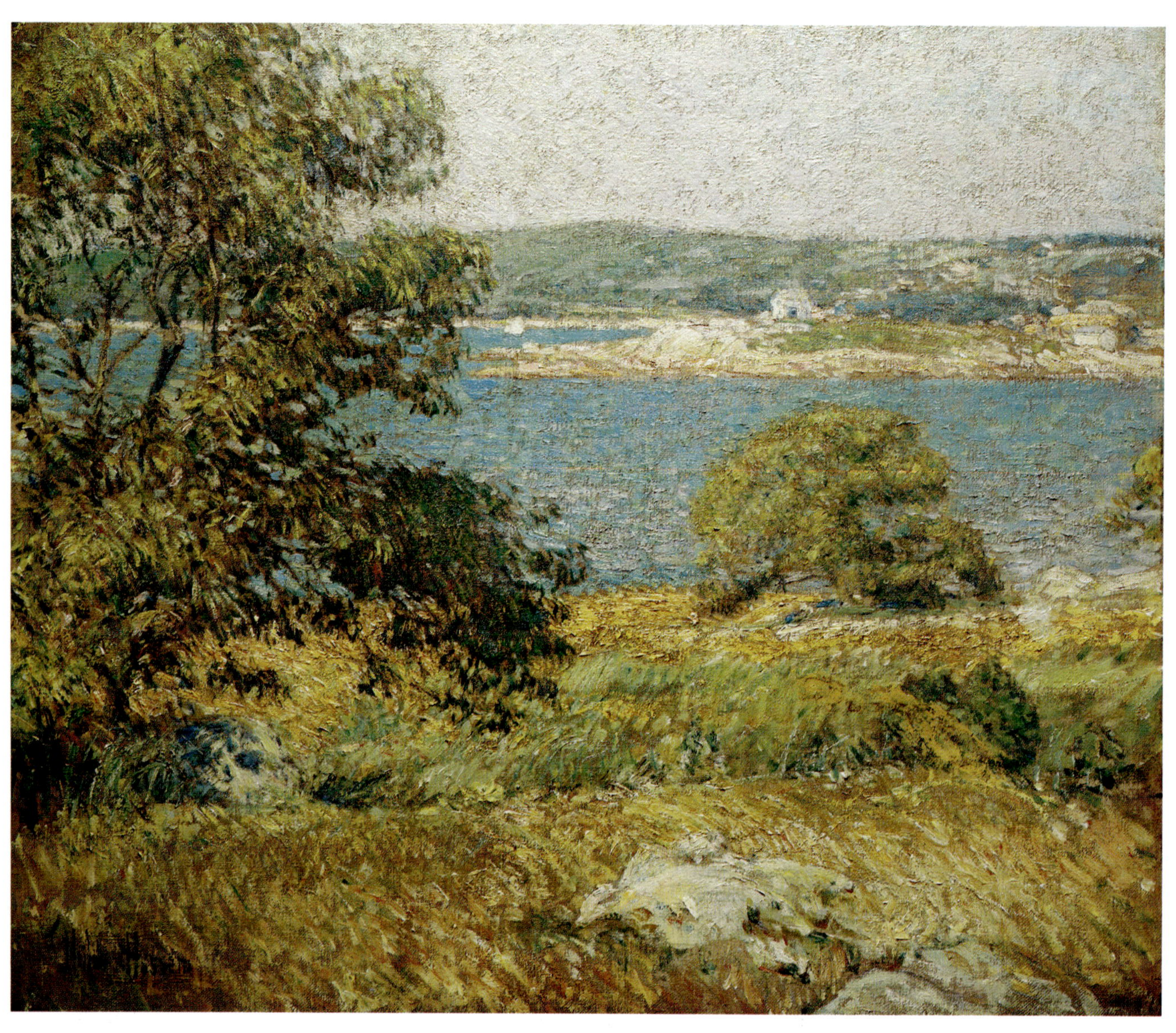

25
CHILDE HASSAM (1859–1935)
Ten Pound Island, c. 1896–1899
Oil on canvas, 20 × 24"
Florence Griswold Museum
Gift of The Hartford Steam Boiler Inspection and Insurance Company

created a powerful image of New England maritime activities in 1901 (see figure 11). Under a gray misty sky, two fishermen, whose powerful frames dominate the composition, haul a huge codfish into a small vessel in the open sea.[12] Depicting the subjects they discovered in such maritime or rural enclaves, these artists offered a vision of life and nature in keeping with the way many Americans imagined and experienced the New England landscape.

Many of the artists who worked in New England were also captivated by old homes, bridges, and other signs of the built environment. Tied to his interest in the New England landscape, Willard Leroy Metcalf painted a number of distinguished colonial homes, including that of Nathaniel Lord in Kennebunkport, Maine (figure 33).[13] Harmoniously connected with the landscape, the old mansion is engulfed by "ancient" trees and flower gardens. Wilson Irvine, a painter associated with the Lyme art colony, also worked on Maine's Monhegan Island depicting the rustic fishing shacks and buildings found there (see figure 46).[14] Another Impressionist painter, Gardner Symons, painted winter landscapes with covered bridges, a structure strongly associated with New England (figure 34). Enshrouded in nostalgia, these images of covered bridges, colonial homes, and old fishing shacks convey a distinctly American sense of place and history closely linked with New England. Many of the works in this exhibition were painted at a time when sweeping changes, including immigration, industrialization, and urbanization, were affecting the nation. For many Americans, the region of New England embodied an enduring history and a sense of stability. Romantic depictions of the scenic beauty of the countryside and its villages symbolized the traditional values that many believed could be found in this historic region.[15]

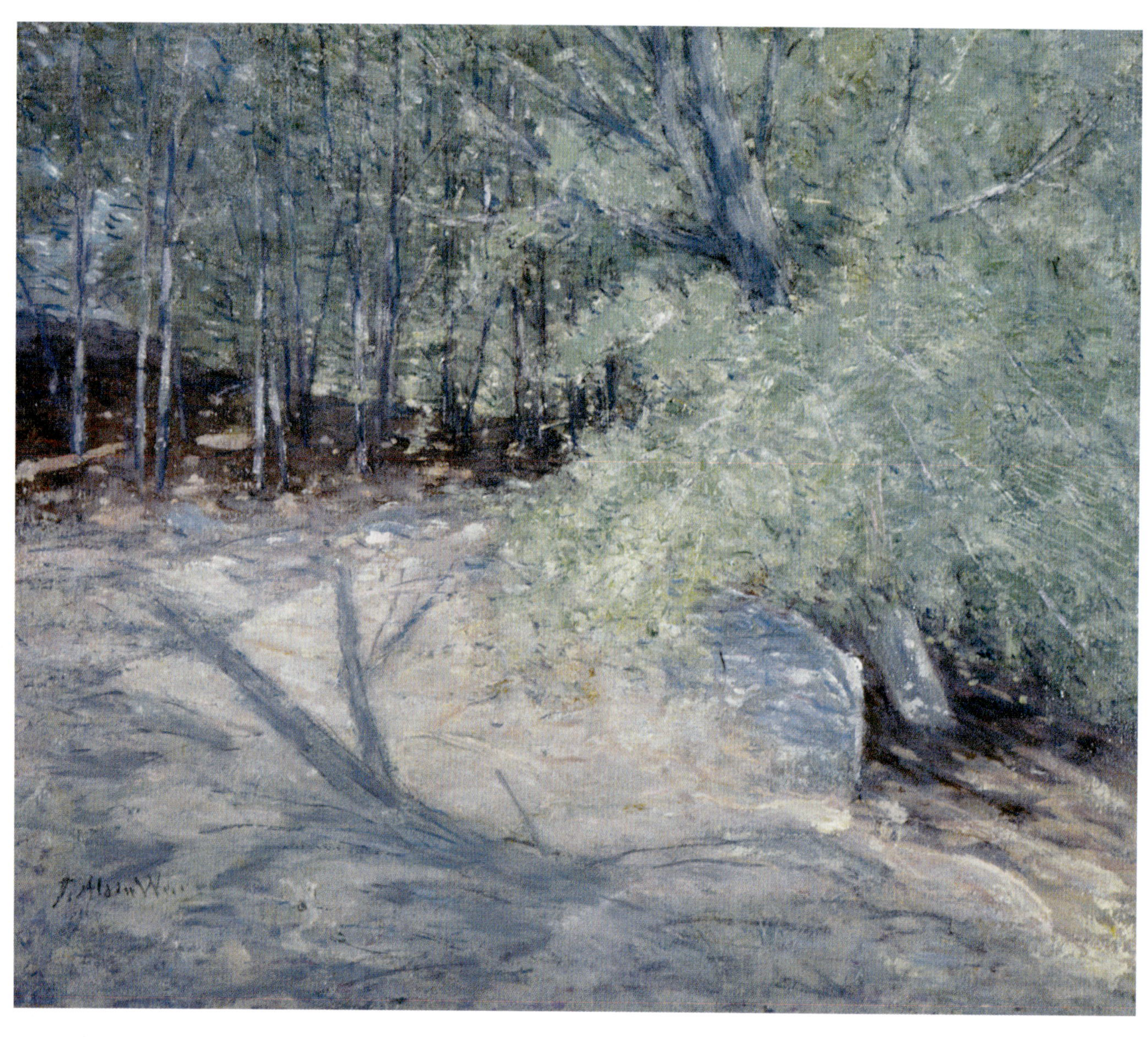

26

JULIAN ALDEN WEIR (1852–1919)

Path in the Woods, n.d. (19th c.)

Oil on canvas, 34 × 40"

Lyman Allyn Art Museum

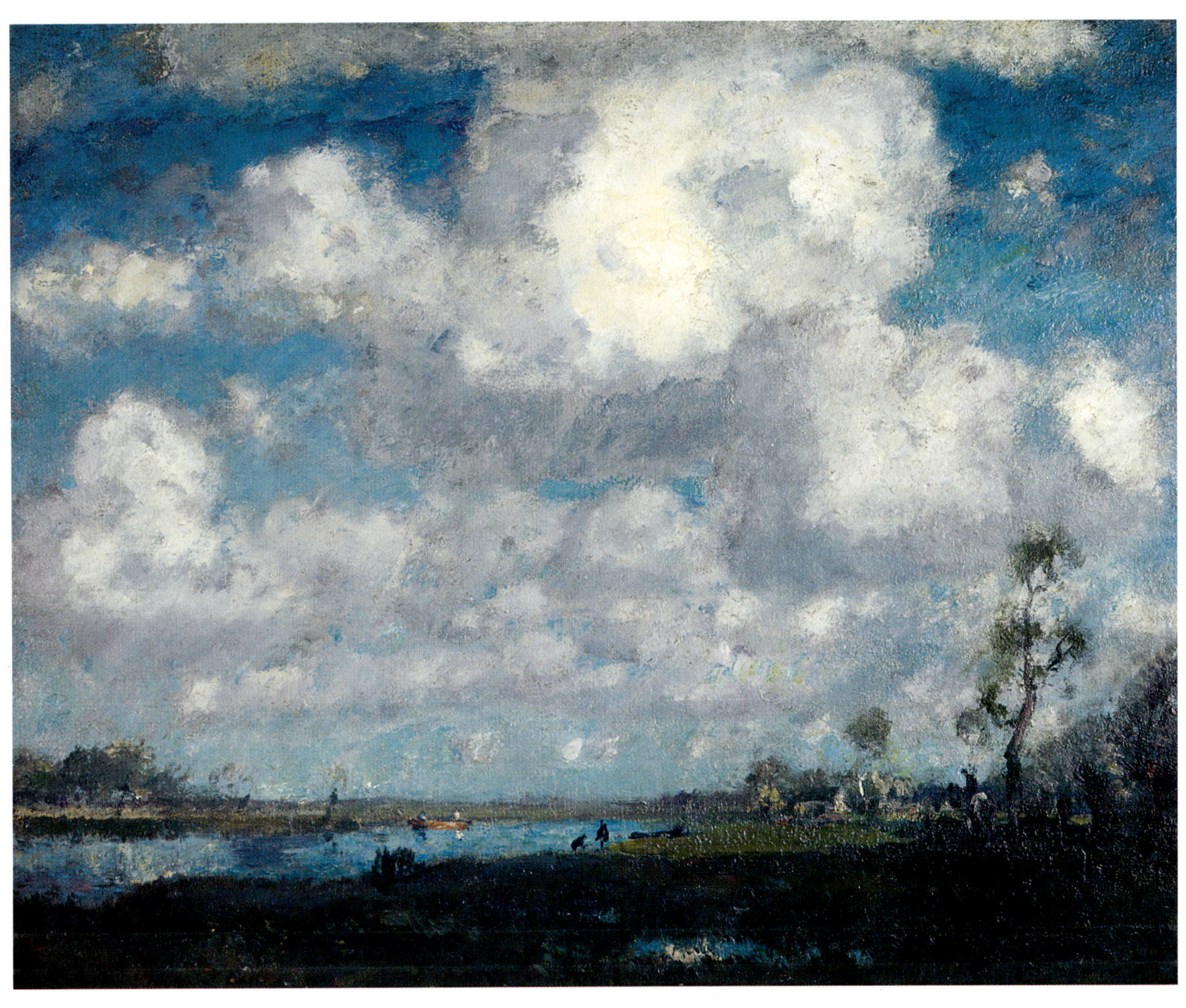

27

HENRY WARD RANGER (1858–1916)

Groton Long Point, 1910

Oil on canvas, 28 × 36"

Florence Griswold Museum

Purchase

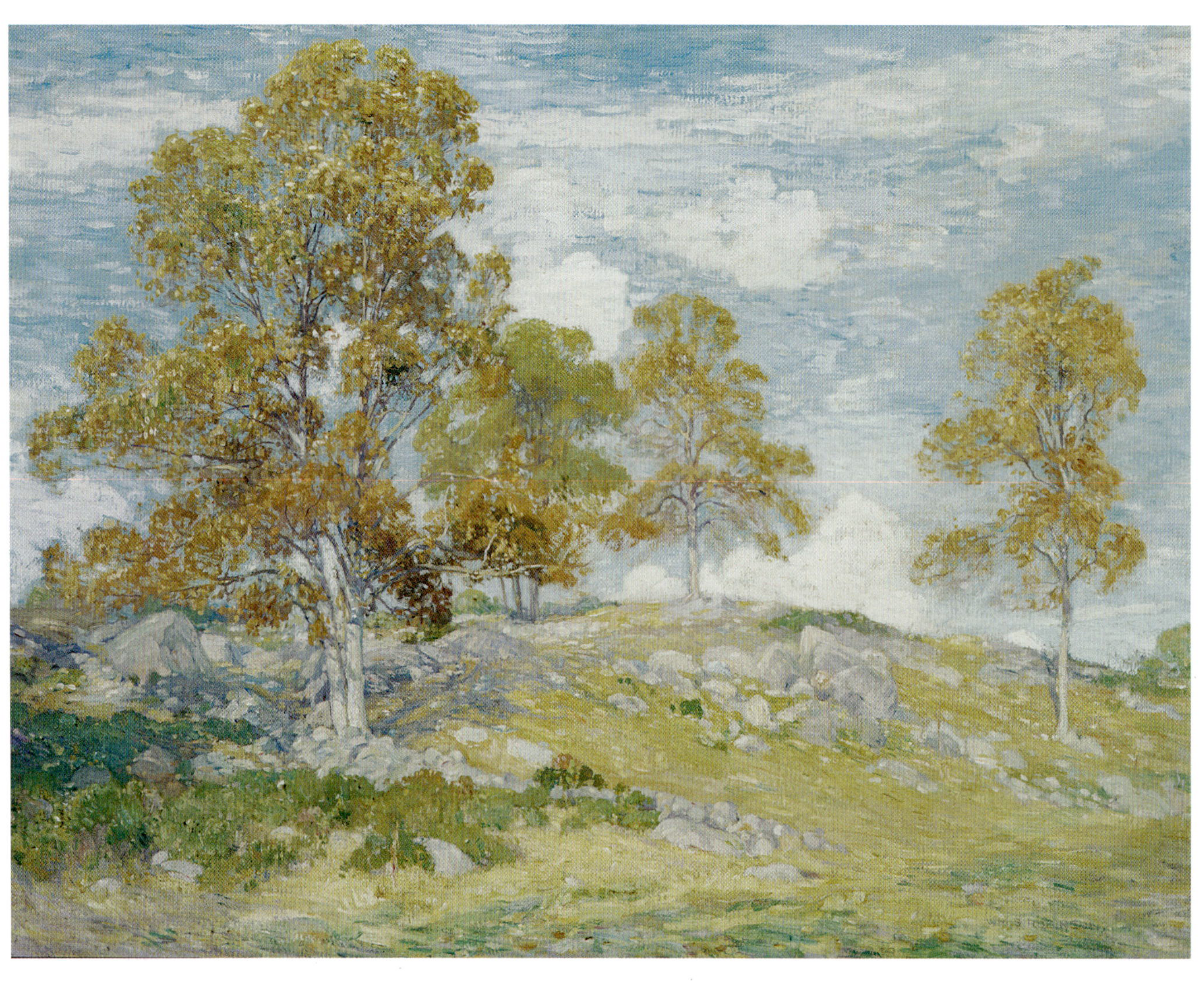

28

WILLIAM ROBINSON (1861–1945)

Autumn Landscape, n.d.

Oil on canvas, 30 × 40"

Florence Griswold Museum

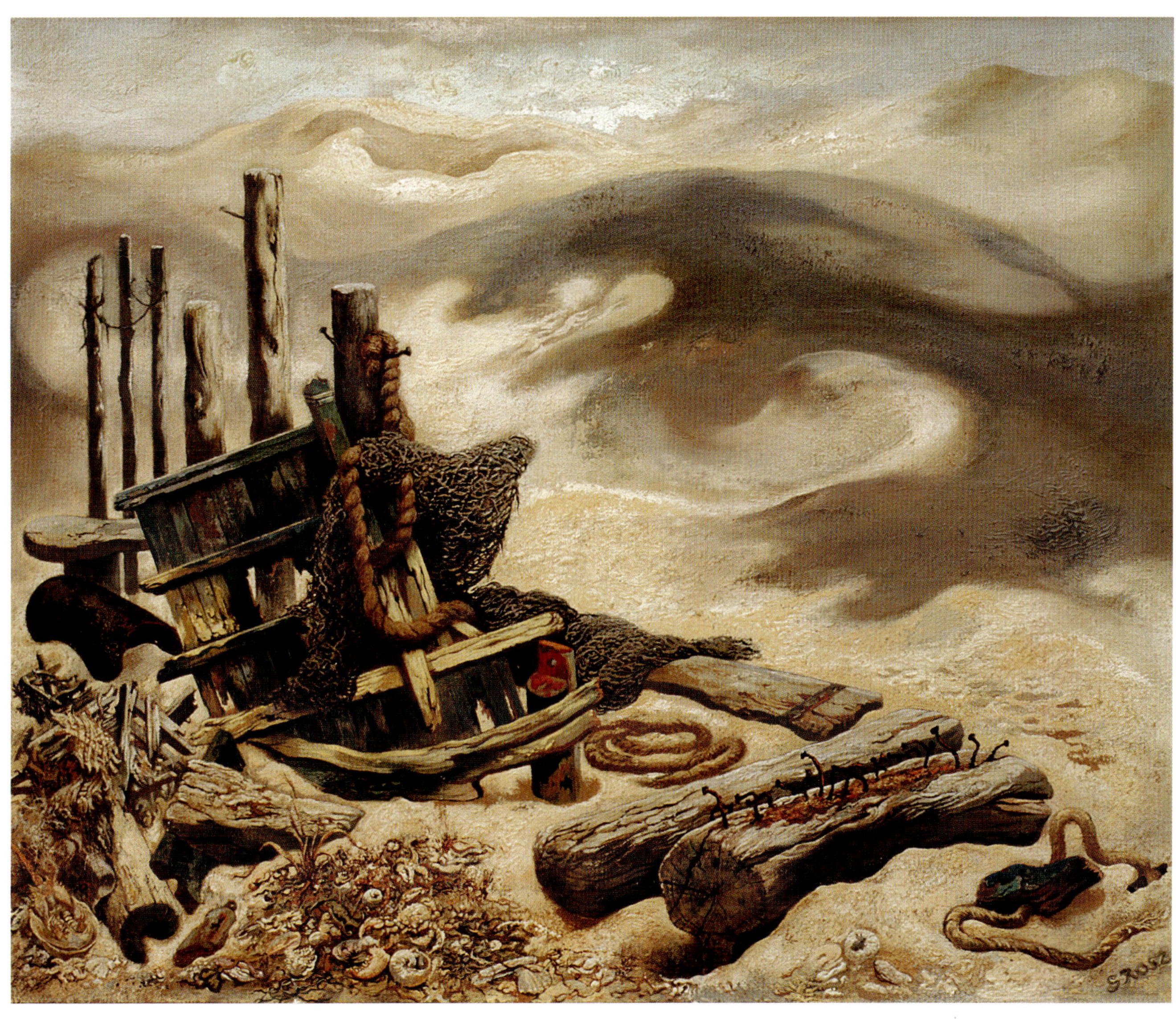

29

GEORGE GROSZ (1893–1959)

Driftwood, 1948

Oil on canvas, 28½ × 34"

Collection of the Cape Museum of Fine Arts, gift of Mr. & Mrs. Frank J. Wiederman

Courtesy of the Cape Museum of Fine Arts, Dennis, Massachusetts.

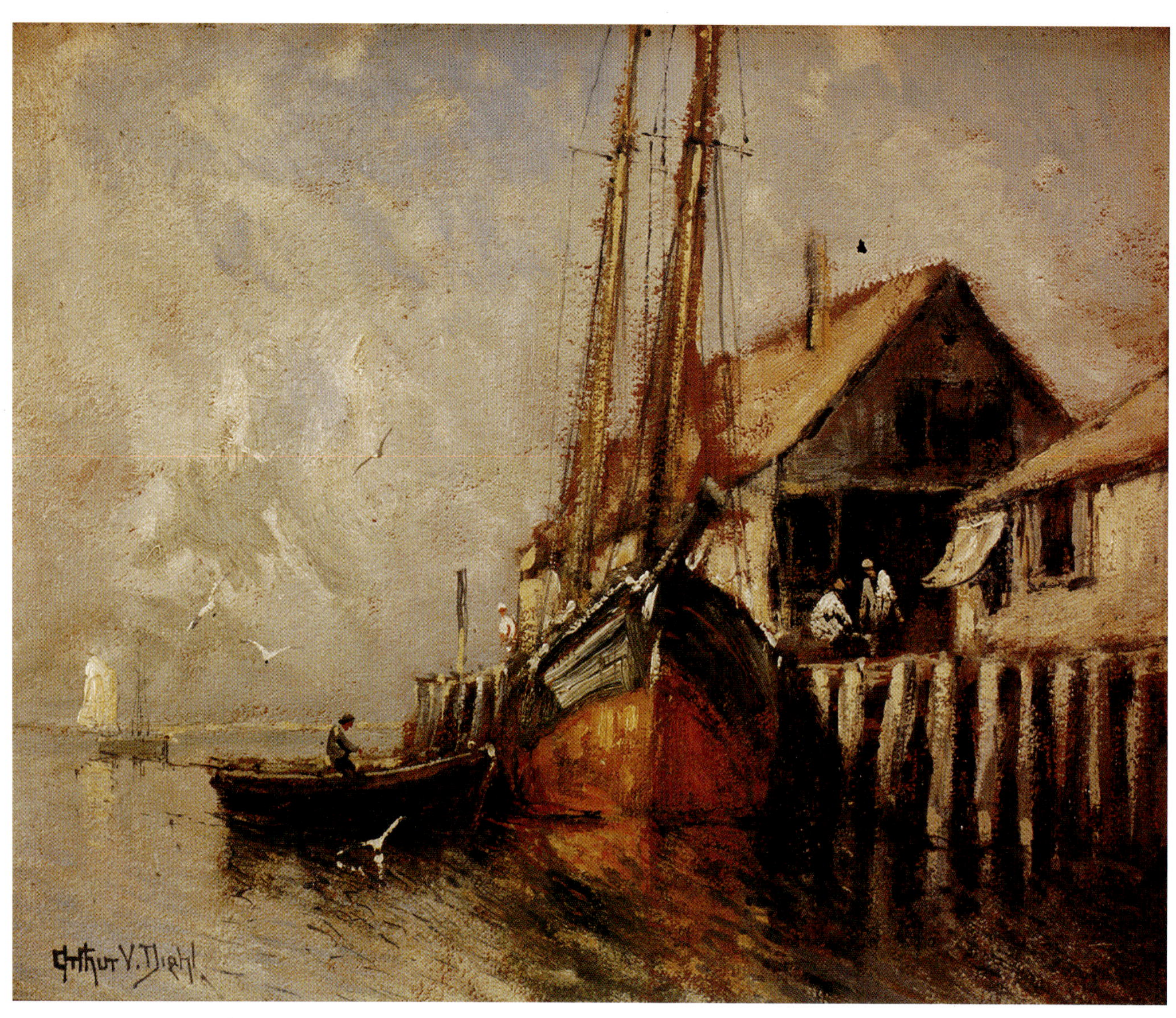

30

ARTHUR DIEHL (1870–1929)

Provincetown Harbor, c. 1920

Oil on board, 18¾ x 13½"

Collection of the Cape Museum of Fine Arts

Gift of Mr. & Mrs. James Couzens

Courtesy of the Cape Museum of Fine Arts, Dennis, Massachusetts.

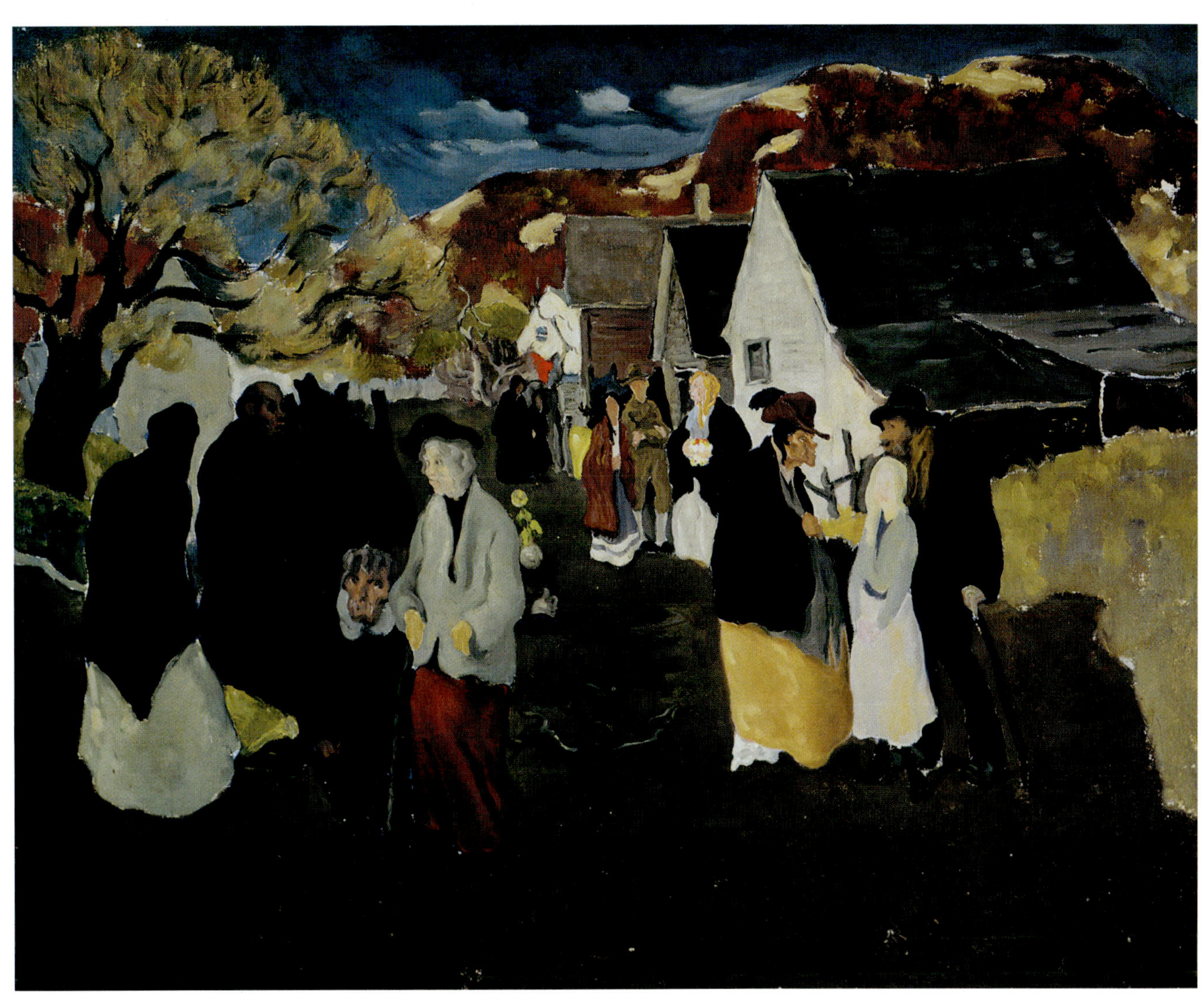

31
ROSS MOFFETT (1888–1971)
Back Street Provincetown, 1917
Oil on canvas, 39¼ × 49½"
Provincetown Art Association and Museum

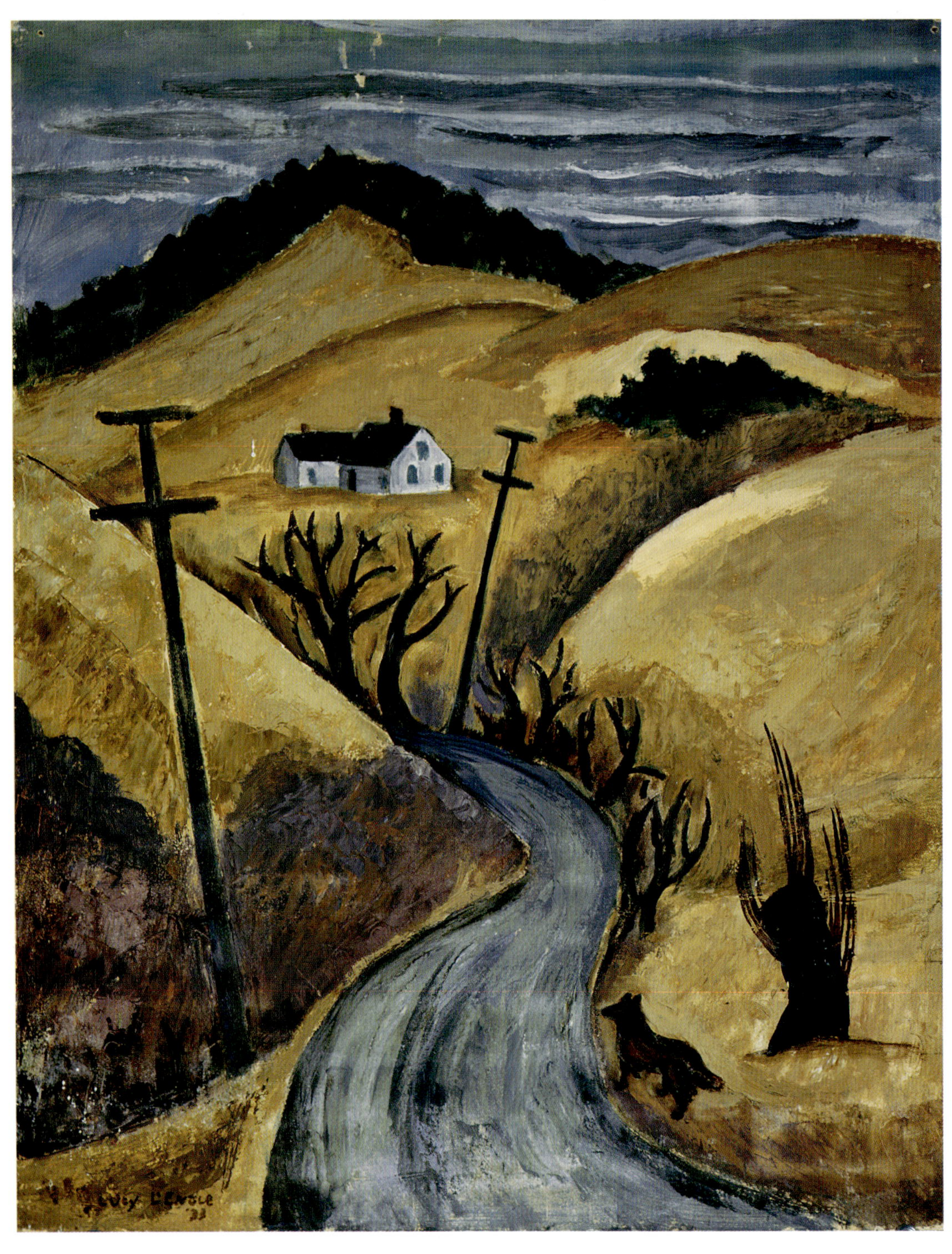

32
LUCY L'ENGLE (1884–1957)
Truro in Winter, 1933
Oil on board, 20 × 16"
Provincetown Art Association and Museum

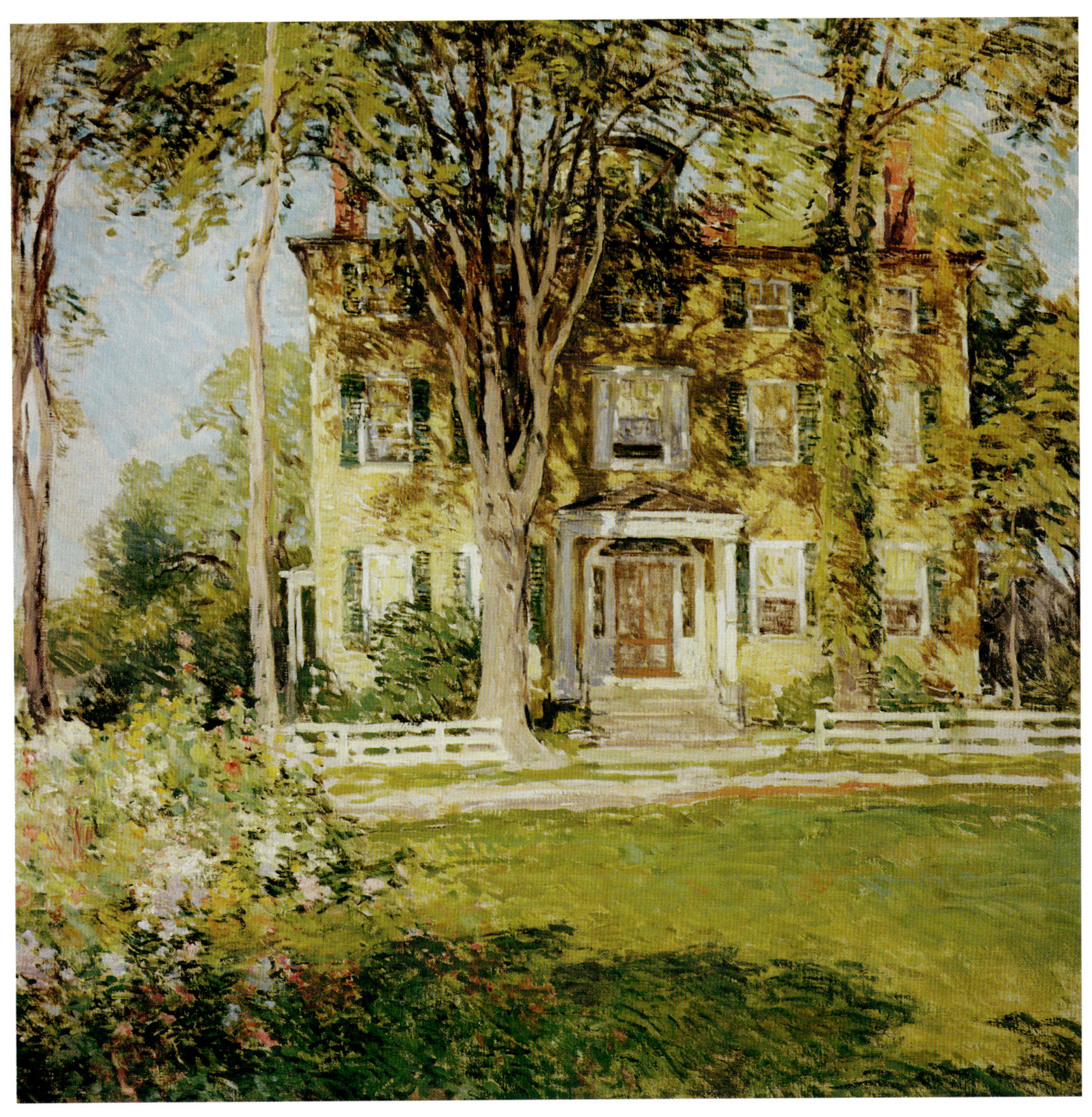

33

WILLARD LEROY METCALF (1858–1925)

Captain Lord House, Kennebunkport, Maine, c. 1920

Oil on canvas, 36 × 36"

Florence Griswold Museum

Gift of Mrs. Henriette Metcalf

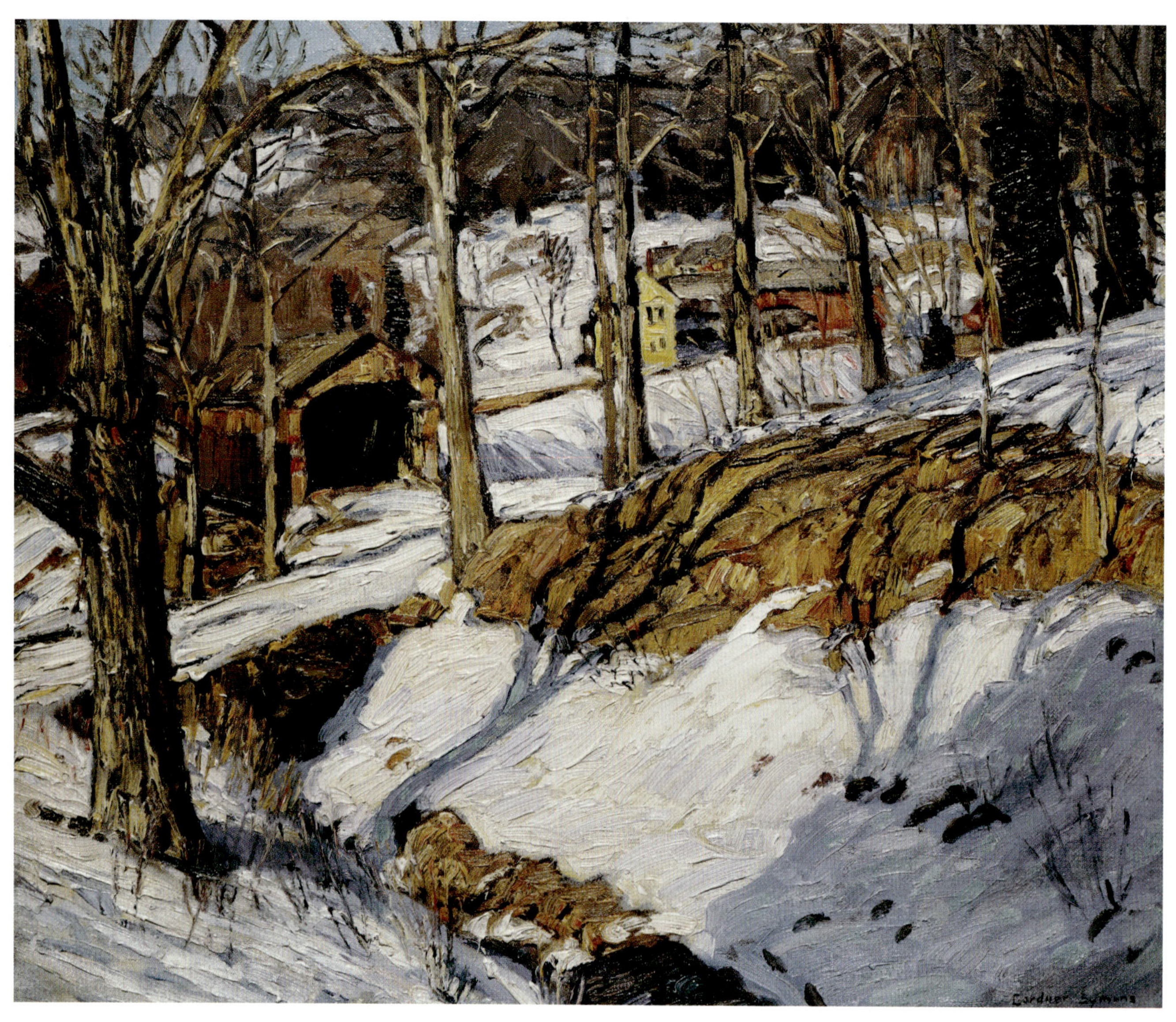

34

GARDNER SYMONS (1861–1930)

Covered Bridge, 1900–1920

Oil on canvas, 25 × 30"

ACM 78.01

Courtesy Art Complex Museum

Modern Voices in New England

New England continued to inspire artists during the twentieth century, and many of these painters were informed by European modernism and new modes of creative expression. Karl Anderson, who moved to Westport, Connecticut, in 1912, often painted in the symbolist style, taking his subjects from Christianity and classical mythology. *Children at a Well* (figure 35), with its flattened spatial relations, saturated colors, and dreamlike treatment exemplified a trend in early American modernism. George Bellows, after experiencing modern art at the 1913 Armory Show, began to employ more vivid colors as in his view of John Tom's farm on Matinicus Island, Maine (figure 36).[16] Closely connected with the avant-garde Stieglitz circle of artists, John Marin approached the subjects he encountered in Maine in an abstract manner (figure 37).[17] As twentieth-century audiences became familiar with modern abstraction and design, many were drawn to the work of untrained or folk artists such as Grandma Moses, whose views of rural Vermont and New York continue to delight audiences today (see figure 44).[18]

Artists also turned to industrial and urban subjects during the twentieth century.[19] Marion Huse, for example, painted the mill in the Berkshire village of Shelburne Falls, Massachusetts, in 1929 (figure 38). The little-known Elsie Rowland Chase, who painted her family and friends, documented the factory her husband owned in Waterbury, Connecticut (figure 39). Another artist, Beatrice Cuming, engaged herself with subjects of modern life, capturing the energy of a Saturday night in New London, Connecticut, during the 1930s (figure 40). Despite these industrial and urban views of the region, the idyllic and gentle landscape of New England continued to captivate both artists and audiences alike throughout the twentieth century. Like others before them, Edward Hopper was drawn to the dramatic headlands overlooking the ocean on Monhegan Island, and Rockwell Kent turned to Mount Monadnock (figures 41, 42).[20] Even the painter Thomas Hart Benton, best known for his regionalist

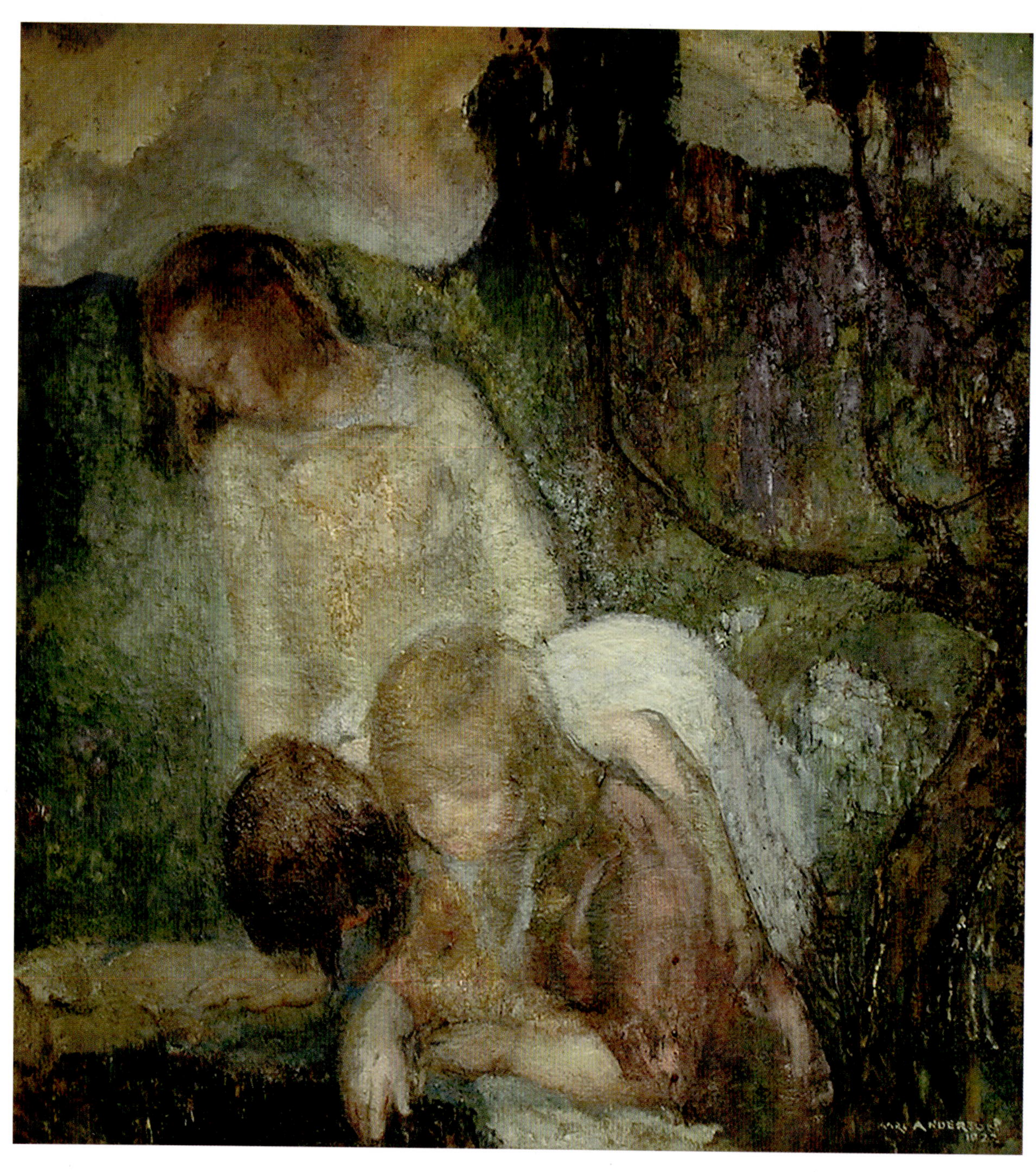

35

KARL ANDERSON (1874–1956)

Children at a Well, 1922

Oil on canvas, 29 × 27"

Collection of Mattatuck Museum, Waterbury, CT

views of life in the Midwest, could not escape the beauty of Cape Cod during the summer months (figure 43).

Envisioning New England reflects this region's enduring appeal to artists during a one-hundred-year time span. Together these diverse works allow us to consider the artists' interpretations of the subjects they encountered while living and working in New England. The styles in which they worked and the subjects they chose to depict may have changed through the decades, but the intrigue that this region had for artists remained constant. Exploring the story of the American artist in New England, this exhibition presents a portrait of the region's creative history and, in so doing, celebrates the collections of the Consortium of New England Community Art Museums.

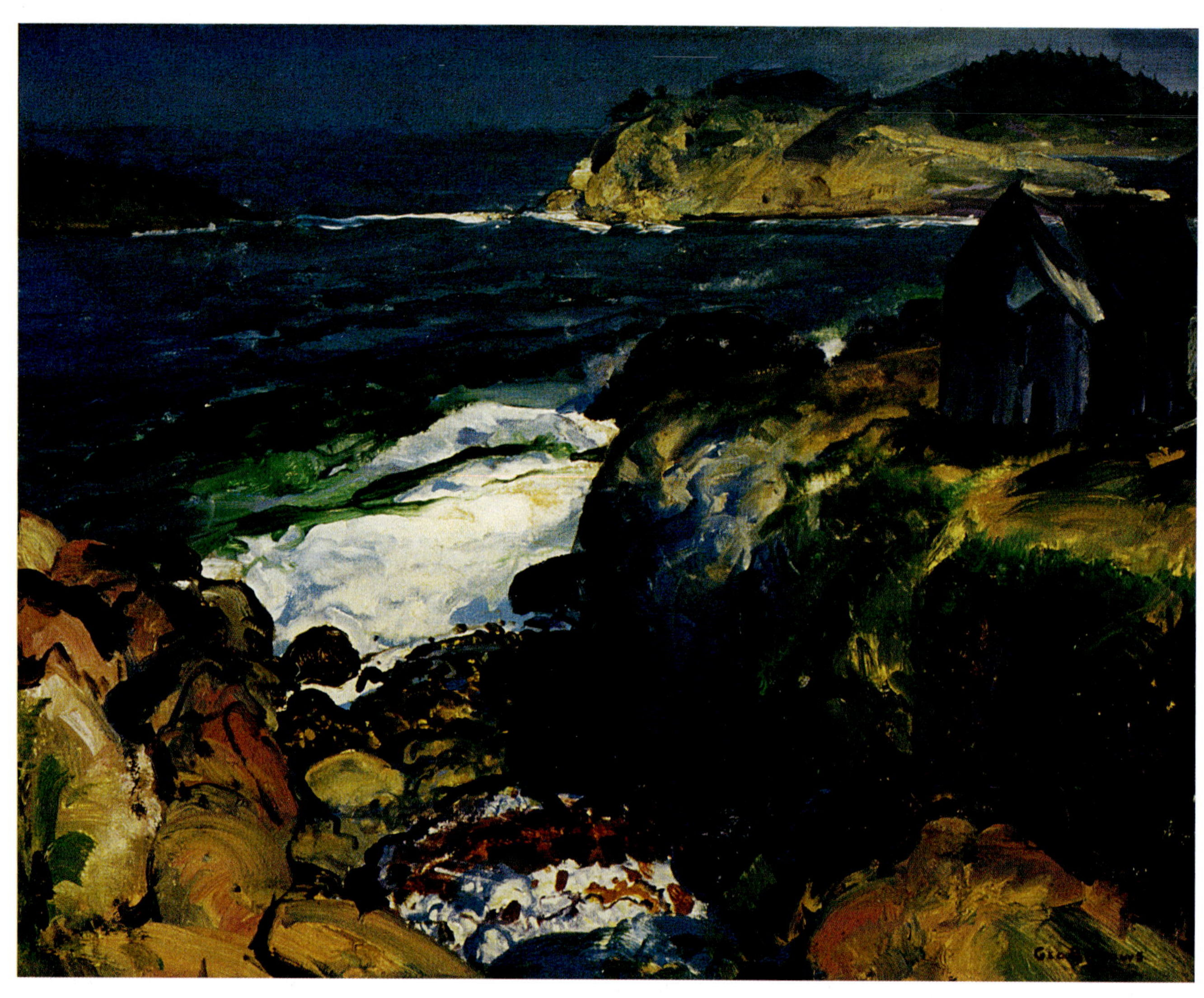

36

GEORGE BELLOWS (1882–1925)

Farm of John Tom, 1916

Oil on canvas, 22 × 28"

ACM 53.8

Courtesy Art Complex Museum

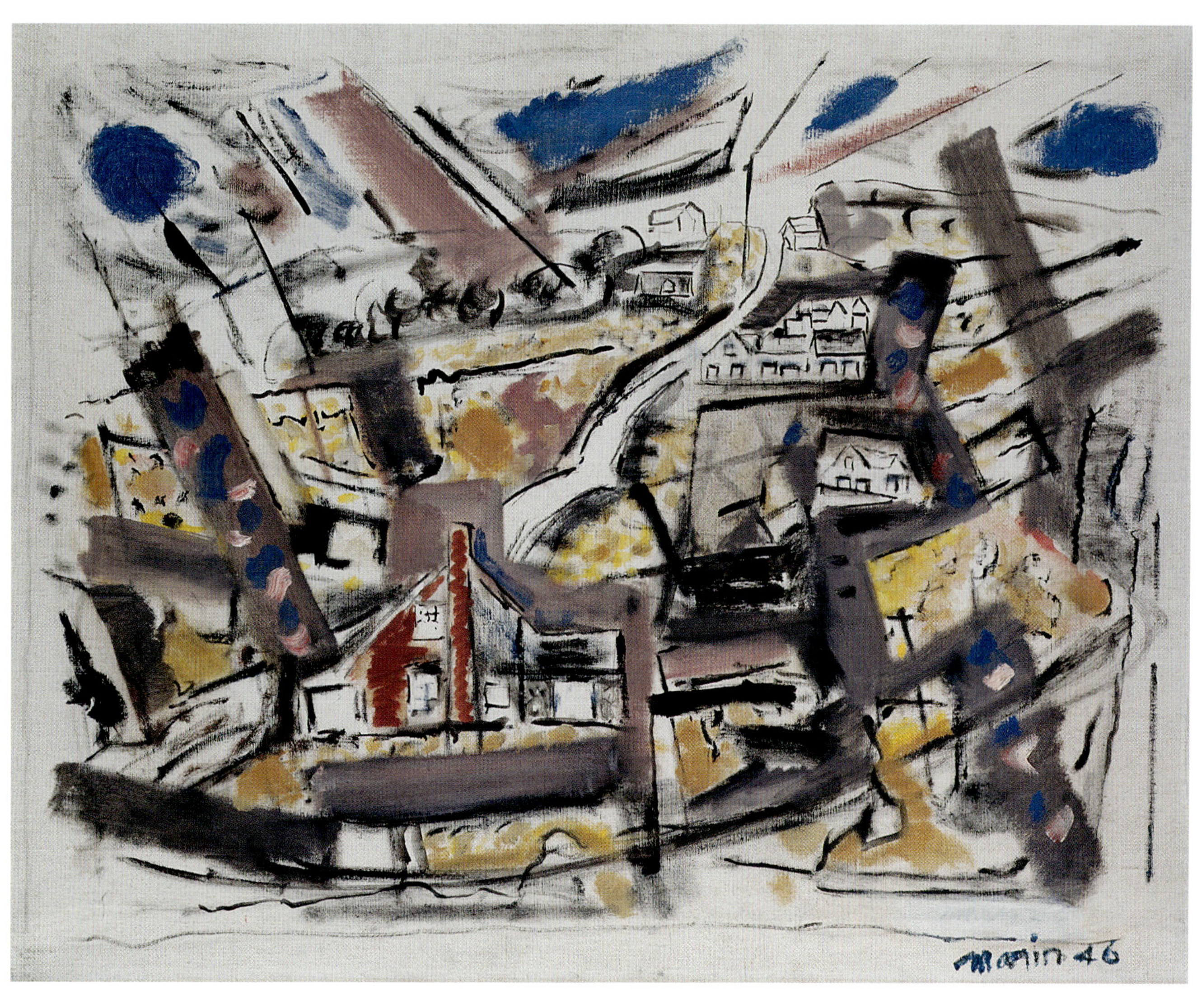

37

JOHN MARIN (1870–1953)

On the Road to Addison, Maine, No. 2, 1946

Oil on canvas, 23 × 29¾"

Collection of the Farnsworth Art Museum

Museum purchase in memory of Thomas Gardiner, 1995

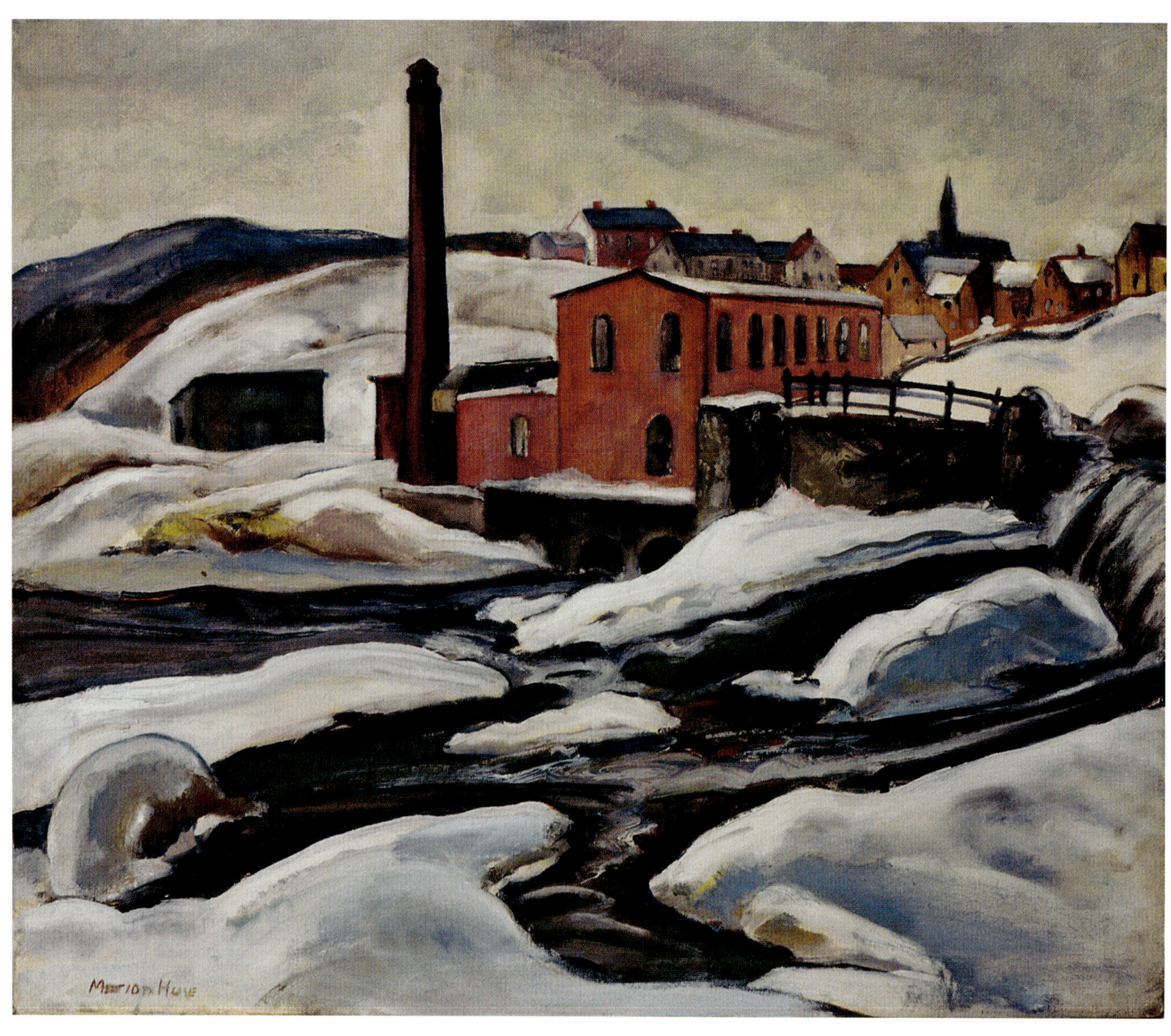

38

MARION HUSE (1896–1967)

Mill at the Falls, 1929

Oil on canvas, 24 × 30"

Signed: lower left: Marion Huse

Exhibited: North Shore Art Association, Gloucester, Massachusetts, *7th Annual Exhibition*, 1929

Fuller Museum of Art, *Marion Huse: An Artist's Evolution*, 1985

Work courtesy of the Fuller Museum of Art, Brockton, MA

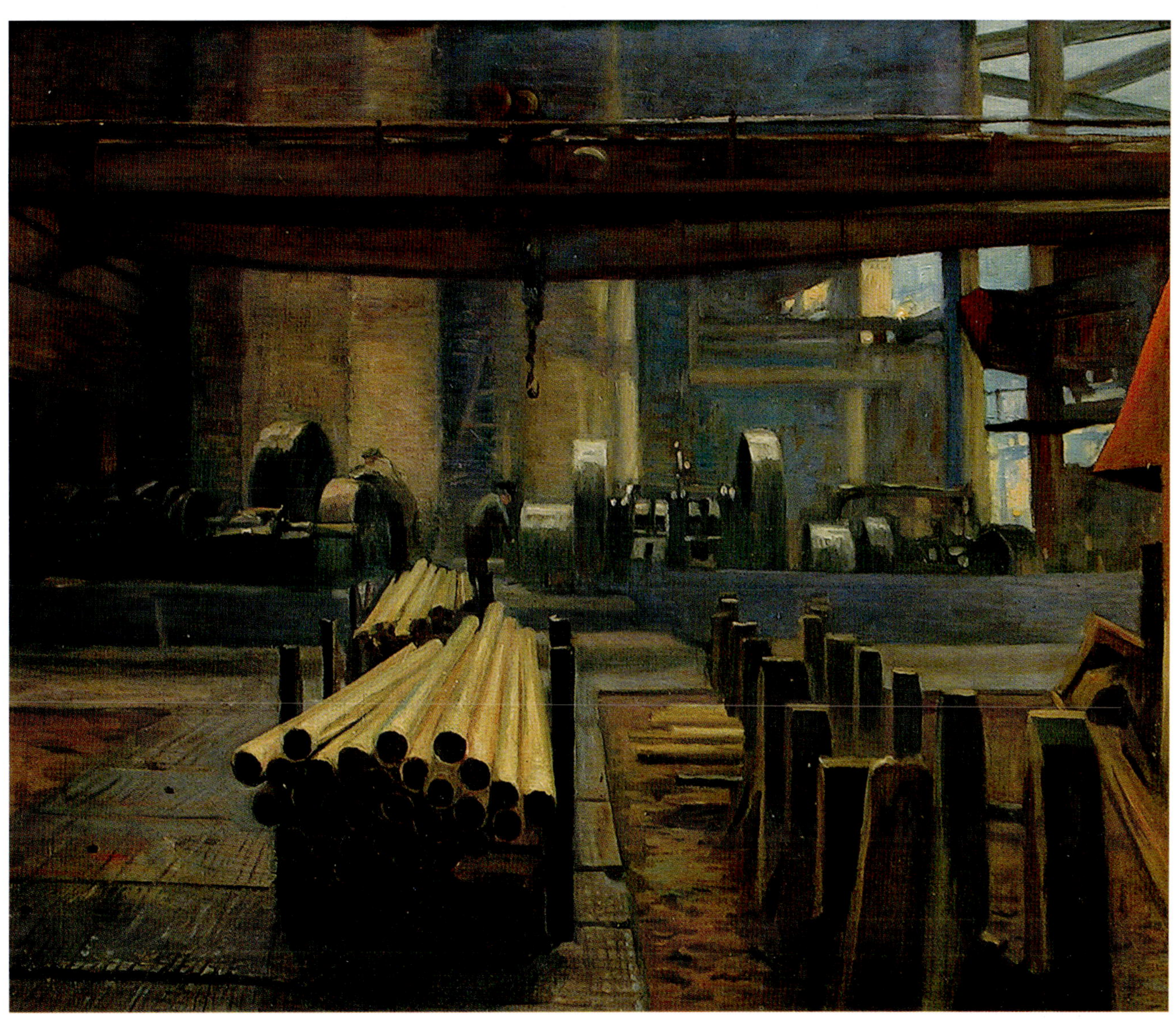

39
ELSIE ROWLAND CHASE (1863–1937)
Chase Rolling Mill, n.d.
Oil on canvas, 24 × 30"
Collection of Mattatuck Museum, Waterbury, CT

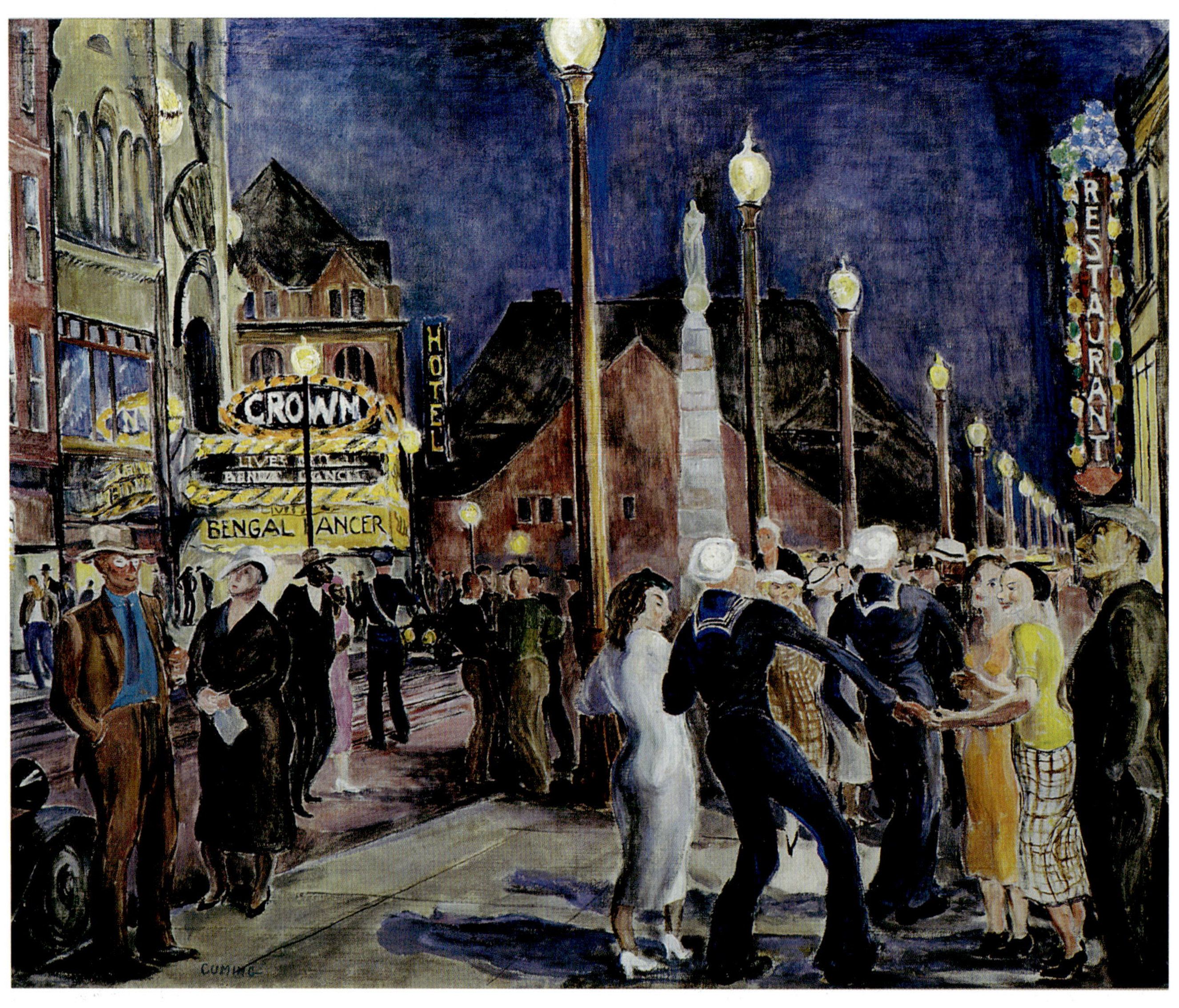

40

BEATRICE CUMING (1903–1975)

Saturday Night New London, 1938

Oil on canvas, 32 × 38¾"

Lyman Allyn Art Museum

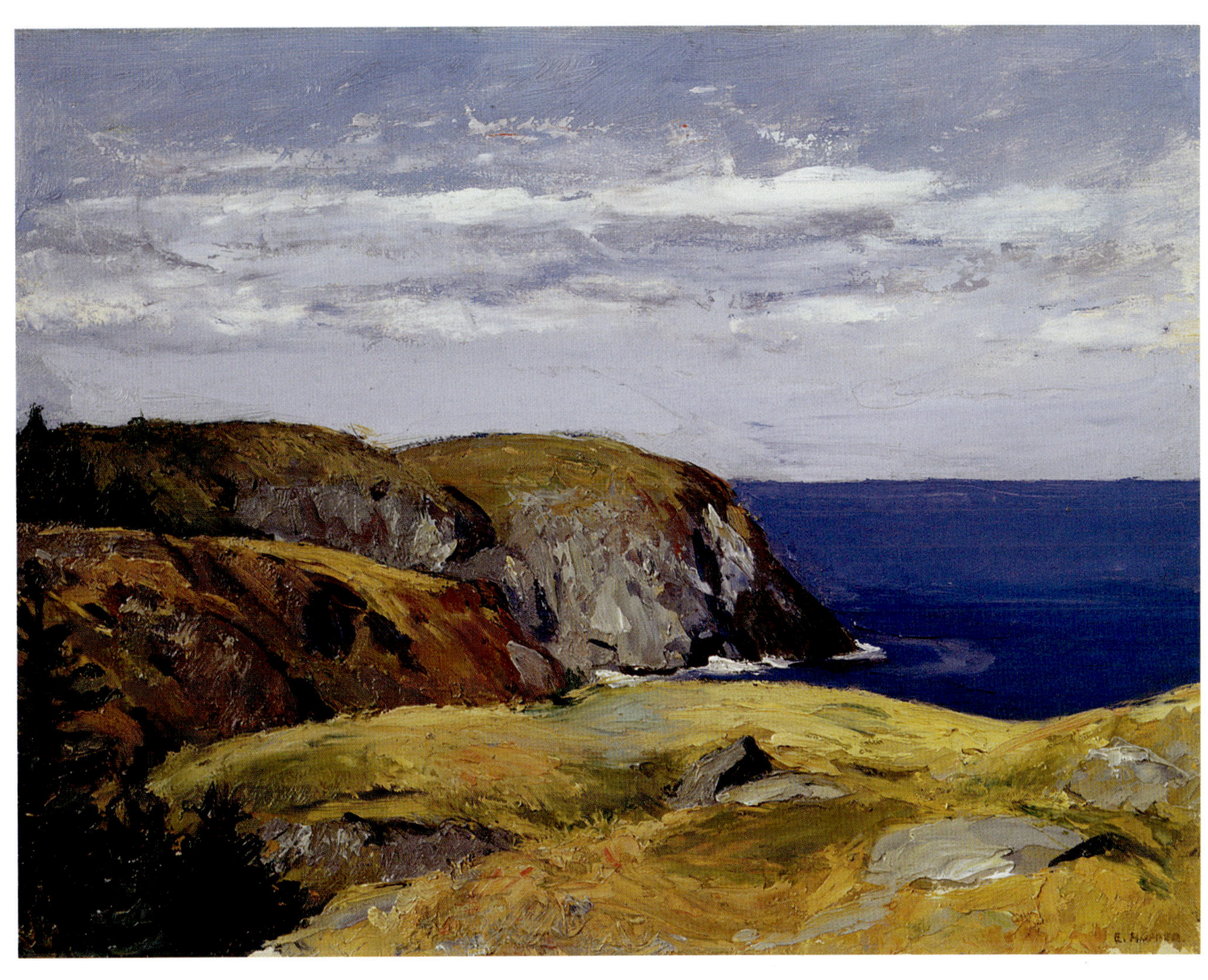

41

EDWARD HOPPER (1882–1967)

Blackhead, Monhegan, c. 1918

Oil on panel, 11½ × 16"

Collection of the New Britain Museum of American Art

Gift of Olga H. Knoepke

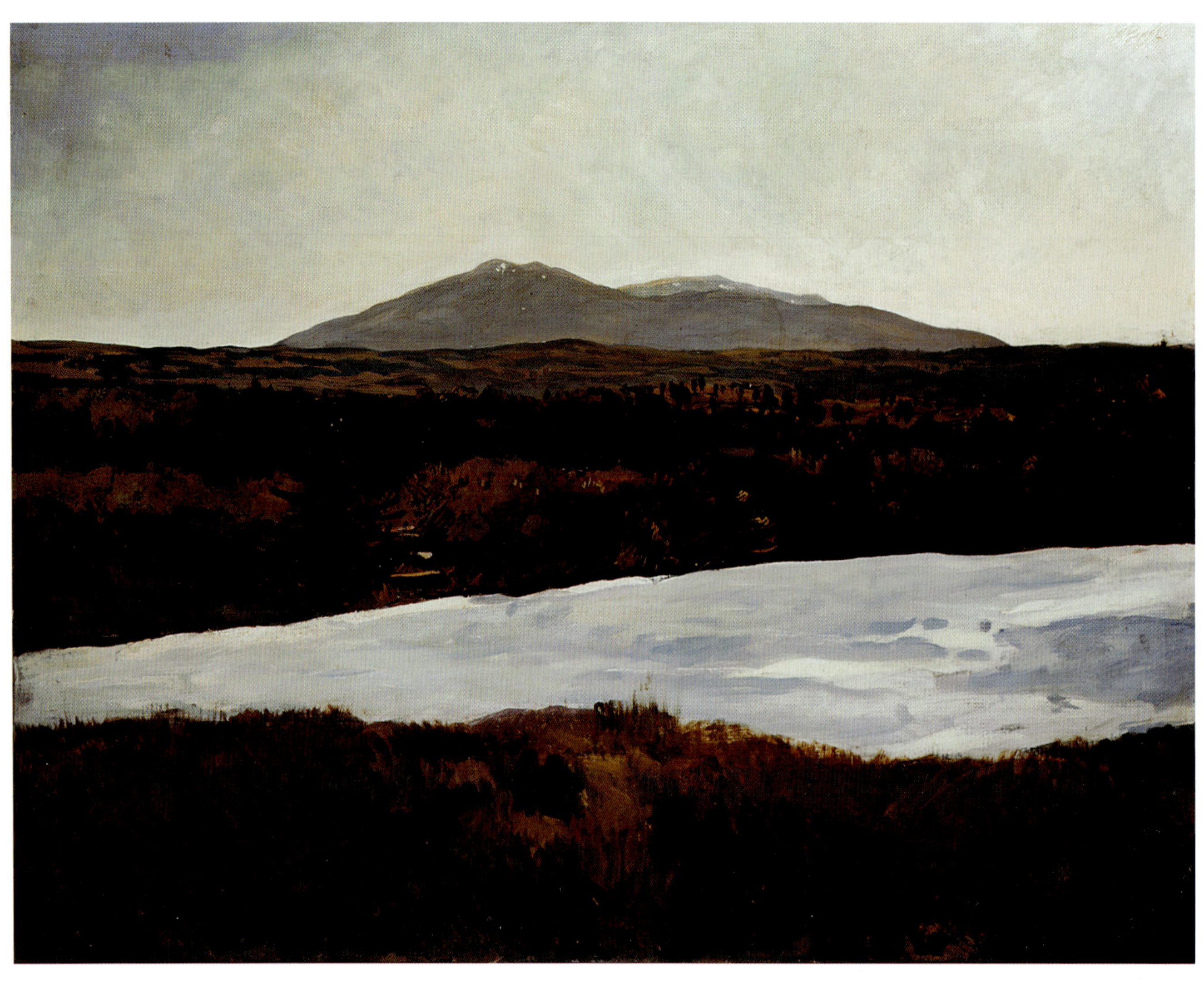

42

ROCKWELL KENT (1882–1971)

Monadnock Afternoon, 1909

Oil on canvas, 34 × 44"

Collection of the Fitchburg Art Museum

Gift of Mrs. Paul Mellon in memory of her grandfather Arthur H. Lowe, 1983.69

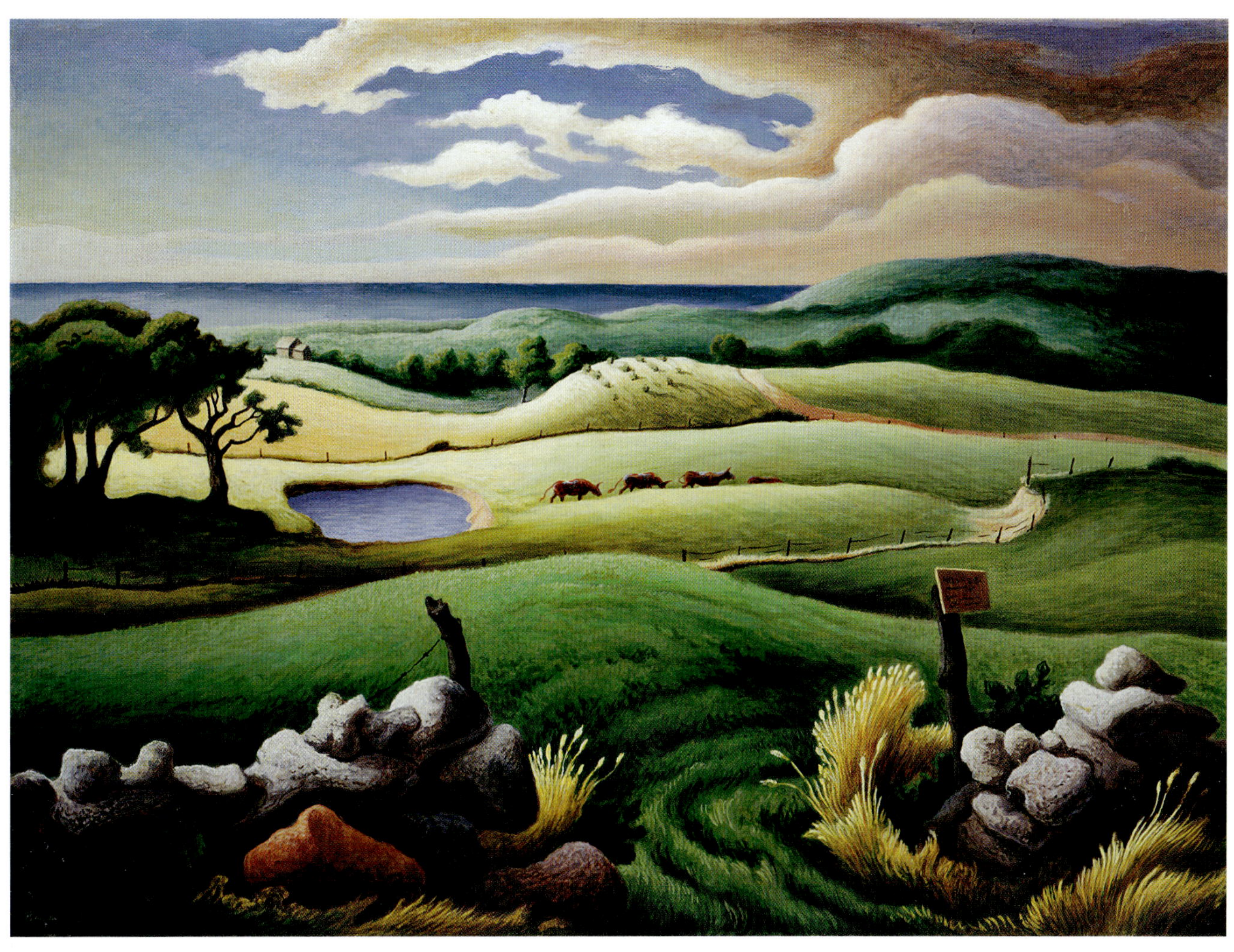

43

THOMAS HART BENTON (1889–1975)

Keith Farm, Chilmark, 1955

Oil on board, 21¾ x 29"

Signed and dated lower left: Benton 55

Gift of Mr. and Mrs. E. Bradford Keith, 1999.2

Work courtesy of the Fuller Museum of Art, Brockton, MA

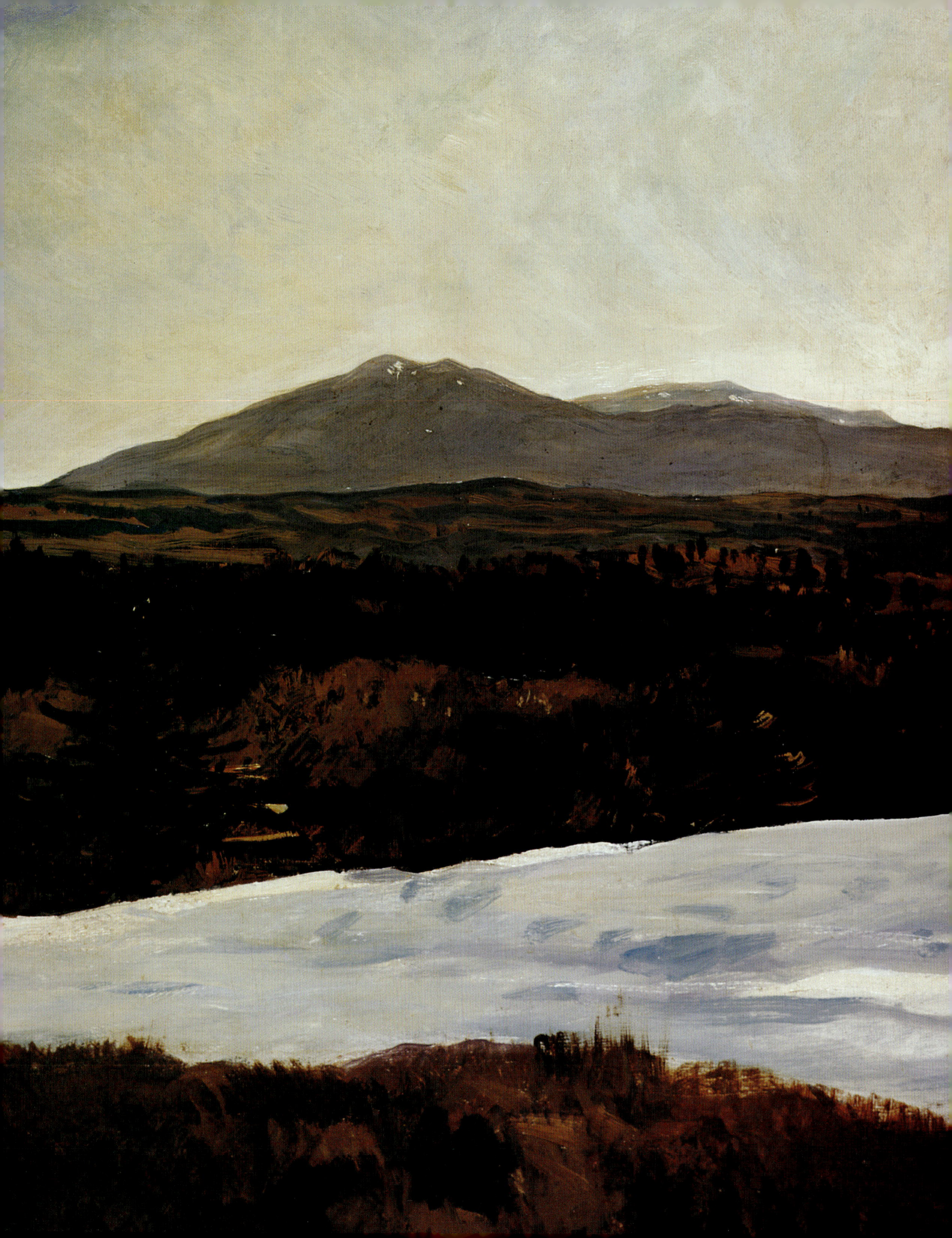

The Legacy Lives

The Story of Our Museums

Compiled and edited by

STEPHANIE N. UPTON

Project Director
Executive Director, Consortium of New England Community Art Museums

❦ *Envisioning New England: Treasures from Community Art Museums* is a collaborative effort of fourteen midsize, community art museums in five New England states. These museums are members of the Consortium of New England Community Art Museums, a group founded in 1993 to broaden the impact of the individual organizations by sharing resources and inviting collaboration. Member institutions share the belief that the community museum plays a unique and valuable role in the cultural landscape of New England. They foster and promote the arts and humanities as a unifying force in a changing society by providing direct access to art and historical artifacts to people within the context of their own communities and beyond. Consortium museums collect, preserve, and exhibit objects, bring outstanding artists and scholars to their publics, and facilitate the teaching of arts and humanities in local school systems.

Loans to the *Envisioning New England* exhibition represent only a few of the art treasures to be found in each museum's collection. Their collections range from antiquities to contemporary works of today, and their programs appeal to the many interests and ages of diverse audiences. The museums offer visitors unique settings for the exploration and enjoyment of art. Each, in its own special way, "celebrates the role of visual arts in the community."

ART COMPLEX MUSEUM

189 Alden Street
Duxbury, Massachusetts 02331
781–934–6634
http://www.artcomplex.org

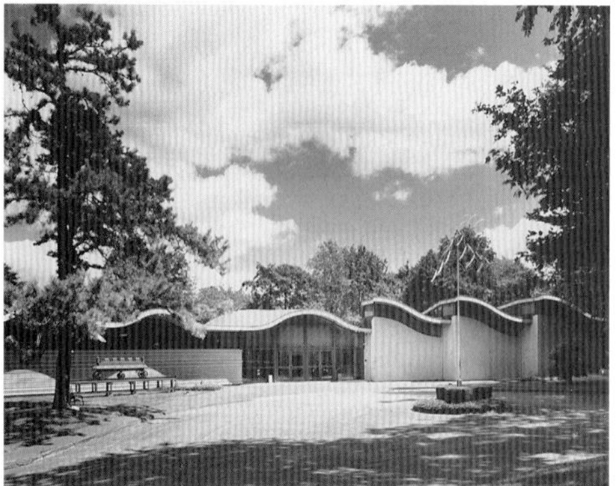

The Art Complex Museum, located in the historic town of Duxbury, thirty-three miles south of Boston, is a center for regional arts and houses the impressive collection of the Carl A. Weyerhaeuser family. The unique venue truly offers visitors an inviting place for "viewing and learning about art in an intimate and comfortable setting," as the Weyerhaeuser family wished.

The history of the museum is interwoven with that of the Weyerhaeusers. Carl Weyerhaeuser, grandson of the founder of the lumber business, was offered an expensive Packard as a graduation gift when he completed his studies at Harvard University. He chose a Rembrandt print, *The Descent from the Cross by Torchlight*, instead of the automobile. Weyerhaeuser was drawn toward works of art on paper, particularly European and American prints. Soon his collecting interests grew to include Shaker furniture, American paintings, and Asian art.

Edith Weyerhaeuser encouraged her husband to build a museum to house this expanding collection and share it with others. The artist Ture Bengtz created an original design, which architect Richard Owen Abbot executed in a contemporary wood and glass building reflecting Weyerhaeuser's interest in honoring his heritage with a "monument to wood." Natural light penetrates glass enclosures looking out on open fields and tall trees. The Bengtz Gallery is leaf-shaped, and both the interior and exterior curves of the building's distinctive roofline have been compared to the ocean waves of seaside Duxbury.

Situated on over thirteen acres of woodland and open fields, the fully accessible museum opened in 1971. Today, highlights of the American painting collection include works by Sanford Gifford, Charles Burchfield, and George Bellows. The museum maintains a close association with the Boston Printmakers, a professional group cofounded by Ture Bengtz, the museum's first director and a friend of the family. The strong print collection of the Art Complex Museum includes images by Albrecht Dürer, Jacques Callot, J. M. W. Turner, Camille Corot, Kaethe Kolwitz, and Rembrandt.

In addition to galleries for changing exhibitions of the permanent collection and traveling collections of contemporary artists, the museum houses the Carl A. Weyerhaeuser Reference Library of over 5,000 publications. On the grounds is a Japanese tea hut, part of the Asiatic Collection, which is used for specifically scheduled tea ceremonies.

The Art Complex Museum offers a year-round schedule of exhibitions, lectures, concerts, classes, demonstrations, and tea ceremonies, fulfilling the founders' vision that their family's many interests be shared with the community.

BENNINGTON MUSEUM

75 Main Street
Bennington, Vermont 05201
802–447–1571
http://www.benningtonmuseum.org

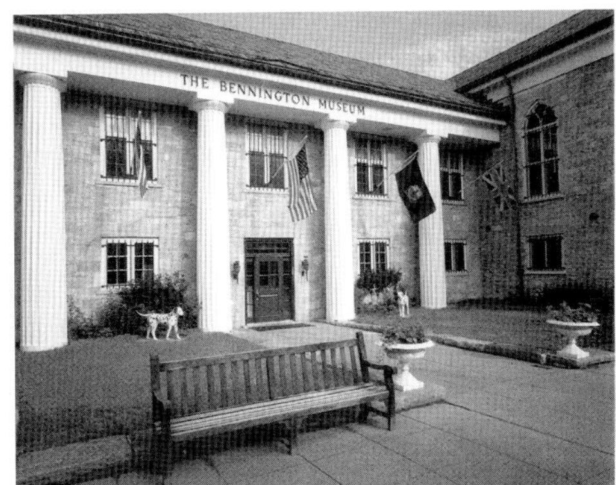

The Bennington Museum is one of the finest regional history and art museums in New England. Its diverse collections reflect the history of early Vermont and historically associated areas of New York and Massachusetts. As the largest and oldest collecting repository in southern Vermont, the museum traces its roots to 1875. It opened at its present site in 1928, expanding in 1937, 1960, and 1999.

Significant early acquisitions included paintings and sculpture by Vermont artists, children's toys, maps, books, and military artifacts. The museum has acquired notable portraits of early settlers by Ammi Phillips; a remarkable townscape by Ralph Earl; newspapers printed in Bennington by one of America's leading abolitionists, William Lloyd Garrison; a Windsor writing-arm chair owned by Ira Allen, a founder of Vermont and author of the state's Constitution; and the world's largest collection of Bennington pottery. Today, artifacts in the collection range in date from the early eighteenth century to the present.

Military history and historical artifacts include the famous Bennington Flag, thought to be one of the oldest Stars and Stripes in existence, uniforms, and firearms, together with early tools, dolls, and toys. The museum has an unsurpassed collection of Bennington pottery on view in a newly redesigned gallery, American paintings and sculpture, and American furniture from the eighteenth and nineteenth centuries. Also on exhibit is the Wasp, a 1925 luxury touring car designed and built by Karl Martin in Bennington.

The museum houses the largest public collection of Grandma Moses paintings in the country (see figure 44) as well as "yarn paintings," art supplies, and the eighteenth-century tilt-top table Moses painted with rustic scenes and used as her easel. In 1972 the museum acquired the Grandma Moses Schoolhouse, which she attended as a child, and moved it from Eagle Bridge, New York, to the grounds of the museum. It now houses exhibitions recording the life and achievements of the artist. Visitors can watch Moses paint and hear her discuss her extraordinary life by viewing a 1955 Edward R. Murrow interview with Moses for his television show *See It Now*.

The museum maintains the largest genealogy library in southern Vermont with a collection of 7,300 books, documents, and primary sources. A research library supports special areas of the museum's collections and includes many general reference sources in the arts and history.

The Bennington Museum's Education Department develops school tours and classroom presentations that support history and art education in public and private schools. The department works in close collaboration with classroom teachers to provide educational services that are not only engaging and fun but educationally sound and in support of the state's new learning standards. Year-round special events include family programs, lectures, and a musical concert series.

The museum is located on Route 9, one mile west of the intersection of Routes 7 and 9 in downtown Bennington, Vermont. It is entirely wheelchair accessible and open year-round.

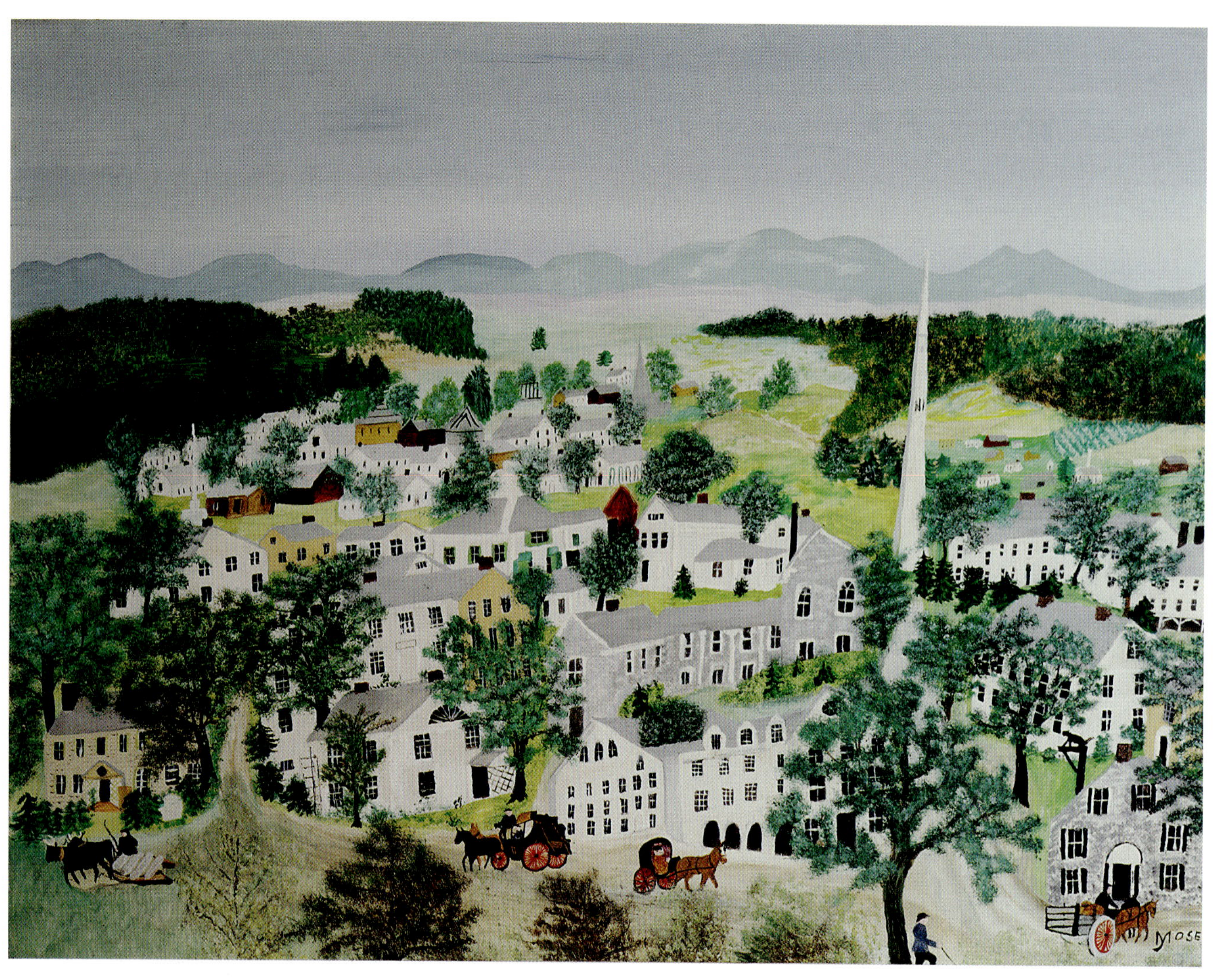

44

GRANDMA MOSES (1860–1961)

Bennington, 1953

Oil on masonite, 18 × 24"

Collection of the Bennington Museum, Bennington, Vermont

CAPE MUSEUM OF FINE ARTS

Route 6A
Dennis, Massachusetts 02638
508–385–4477
http://www.cmfa.org

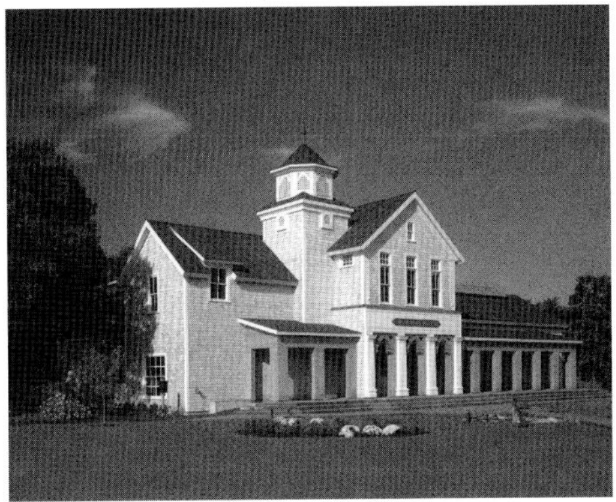

The Cape Museum of Fine Arts celebrates the important role that artists of Cape Cod and the Islands have played in American art since 1899. A group of artists, educators, and community activists founded the museum in 1981 to collect and exhibit works of artists who have been influenced by the Cape and Islands, their people, and their artistic trends and traditions.

The museum collects and shows the work of the Provincetown painters of the early and mid–twentieth century, and of contemporary artists inspired by Cape Cod and its environs. Each year, a number of changing exhibitions highlight works in a variety of media. The nature of the facility provides visitors a particularly intimate and personal experience with the art of this region.

Opened in July 2002, the newly renovated and expanded museum campus has seven fully accessible exhibition galleries, a beautifully landscaped sculpture garden, a research library, a ninety-two-seat auditorium, and a museum shop. The Weny Education Center occupies an 1,800-square-foot addition completed in 2003.

The Cape Museum of Fine Arts is located in the charming village of Dennis, a whaling, shipbuilding, and farming community of yesteryear that offers visitors greeting-card images of a small white church on a village green with a bandstand gazebo. It has antique shops, cafés, and bistros and an old-fashioned ice cream store where all thirty-two flavors are homemade.

The Cape Museum of Fine Arts presents exhibitions, lectures, tours, films, art discovery trips, kids' summer art programs, and other interpretive programs. Its popular weekend film series features art-related as well as independent and foreign films. The museum is on the grounds of the Cape Playhouse Center for the Arts along with the Cape Cinema and the Playhouse Bistro. It is open year-round.

DANFORTH MUSEUM OF ART

123 Union Avenue
Framingham, Massachusetts 01702
508–620–0050
http://www.danforthmuseum.org

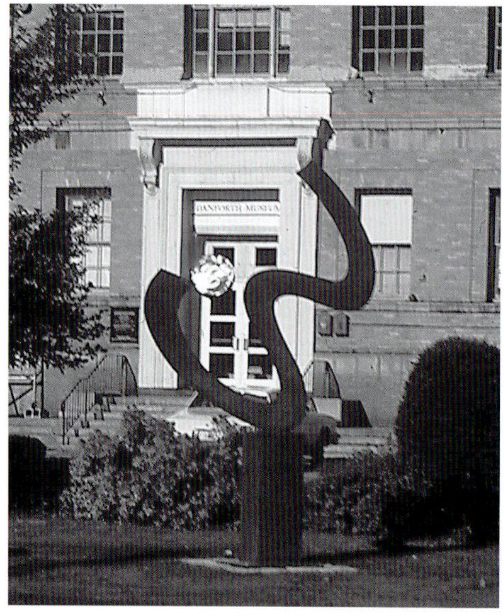

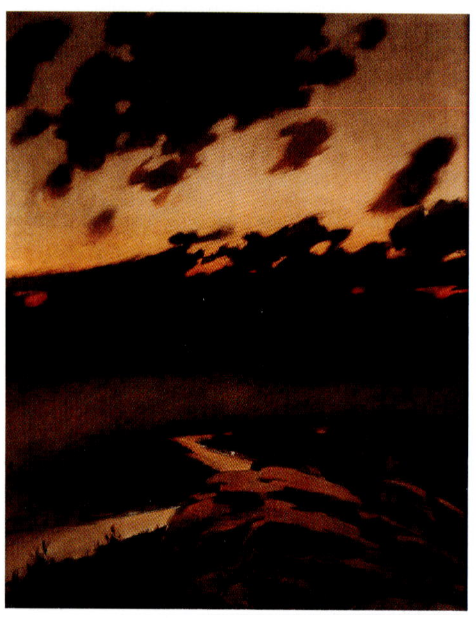

The Danforth Museum of Art, located thirty miles west of Boston, is a vital cultural resource for the local area. Founded in 1975 by a dedicated group of citizens, the museum is a nonprofit, privately supported public art museum committed to the celebration and creation of art. It was named for Thomas Danforth, the original holder of the land grant that is now the Metro West area of Boston.

The permanent collection focuses on American art of the nineteenth and twentieth centuries (figure 45) but includes European masters such as Matisse, Braque, and Picasso. The American artists Gilbert Stuart, James McNeill Whistler, Albert Bierstadt, Yves Tanquy, Karl Knaths, Thomas Hart Benton, and Faith Ringgold are all represented in the museum's holdings. A recent gift from Jean and Kahlil Gibran added over 150 works of art to the museum's collection. Gibran, an accomplished artist, inventor, and writer, personally knew many of the artists whose works are part of this collection.

Each year, the Danforth presents a number of temporary exhibitions of historical and contemporary art. Recently featured artists include Andrew Stevovich, Jaune "Quick-To-See" Smith, David Bakalar, and many other photographers, sculptors, printmakers, and painters. There is also an interactive gallery designed for the museum's youngest audience.

The museum's founders wanted the institution to go beyond the mere presentation of art. They sought opportunities for audiences to respond to artworks. Today, a year-round schedule of classes, concerts, lectures, and tours provides visitors with entertaining and educational experiences in the visual arts, encouraging all ages to "make art part of life."

The Danforth Museum School is an important part of the museum. Every year over five thousand children and adults participate in the more than seventy classes offered at the school. Sculpture, photography, weaving, watercolors—these are just a sampling of the array of classes available. Small classes and quality instruction allow each student to develop his or her potential. Three galleries in the school wing exhibit the work of students and instructors.

An historic 1907 brick school building houses the collections, school, and the Marks Fine Arts Library. The library contains over 10,000 volumes of art reference books and materials. The museum is open year-round, is wheelchair accessible, and is close to major interstate highways.

45
GEORGE H. HALLOWELL (1871–1926)
Sky from Bowlin Camp, c. 1887
Oil on canvas, 30 x 25"
Collection of the Danforth Museum of Art
Gift of Paul and Faith Pigors, 1990.17

FARNSWORTH ART MUSEUM

16 Museum Street
Rockland, Maine 04841
207–596–6457
http://www.farnsworthmuseum.org

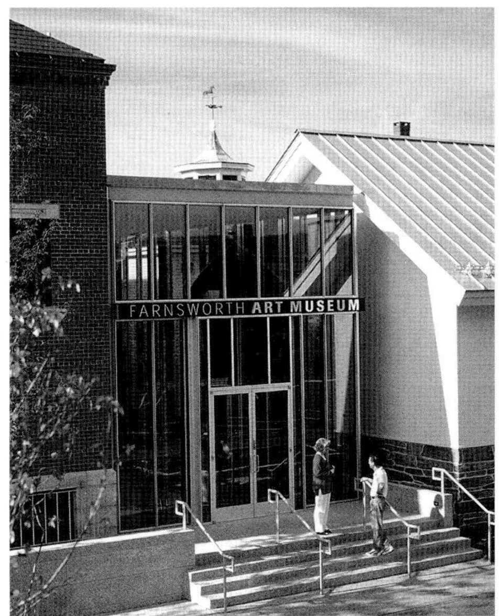

The Farnsworth Art Museum, opened in 1948, is dedicated to the collection, preservation, exhibition, and interpretation of Maine's role in American art. The fully accredited museum is a major art resource for the state of Maine and the northeastern United States.

In 1935, Lucy C. Farnsworth established a trust with the Boston Safe Deposit and Trust Company to create an art museum and library in memory of her father and to ensure the preservation of her family home. In accordance with her will, the bank began to plan an institution that would serve as a cultural center for Rockland, then a rural coastal community. Although construction was delayed until 1946, Robert Bellows (an adviser to the Boston Museum of Fine Arts) was engaged to purchase a collection. He assembled a remarkable collection of nineteenth- and early-twentieth-century works by such American masters as Eastman Johnson, Winslow Homer, Frank Weston Benson, and John Marin.

In its first four decades, the museum advanced Bellows's original focus through judicious acquisitions and numerous exhibitions, staging the first Maine museum exhibitions of the work of Louise Nevelson, Robert Indiana, Neil Welliver, Alex Katz, N. C. Wyeth, Andrew Wyeth, and James Wyeth.

The 1990s saw significant growth and expansion of the museum and its collections. A major bequest brought sixty-six works to the museum, including paintings by Fitz Hugh Lane, George Bellows, and Edward Hopper. Four new galleries in the Jamien Morehouse Wing now showcase the Farnsworth's permanent collections with the exhibition *Maine in America*. The museum houses the nation's second-largest collection of works by the twentieth-century sculptor Louise Nevelson. The Wyeth Center, a remodeled 1870s church across the street from the main museum complex, provides a venue for viewing works by two generations of an American artistic dynasty—N. C. and James Wyeth. The Edwin C. Gamble Education Center houses the Farnsworth's new educational database.

The Farnsworth maintains two historic residences, both circa 1850, representing significant aspects of Maine's cultural history. The Farnsworth Homestead tells the story of upper-class life in nineteenth-century coastal Rockland. The Olson House, in Cushing, represents the precarious rural life of shipmasters and saltwater farmers whose descendants became, for three decades, the subject of Andrew Wyeth's sustained and poignant soliloquy on Christina and Alvaro Olson and their home.

In 2000 the museum published a comprehensive catalogue of its paintings, watercolors, and sculpture collections. The collections serve as the basis for the museum's Arts Initiatives for Maine Schools, a program that serves schoolchildren across the state and in outlying island communities. A year-round calendar of activities including lectures, family programs, films, seasonal celebrations, and changing exhibitions provides visitors with many opportunities to enjoy and learn about art.

The historic and picturesque town of Rockland, Maine, along coastal Route 1, is a major destination for summer tourists. The Farnsworth Art Museum is wheelchair accessible and open year-round.

FITCHBURG ART MUSEUM

Merriam Parkway
Fitchburg, Massachusetts 01420
978-345-4207
http://www.fitchburgartmuseum.org

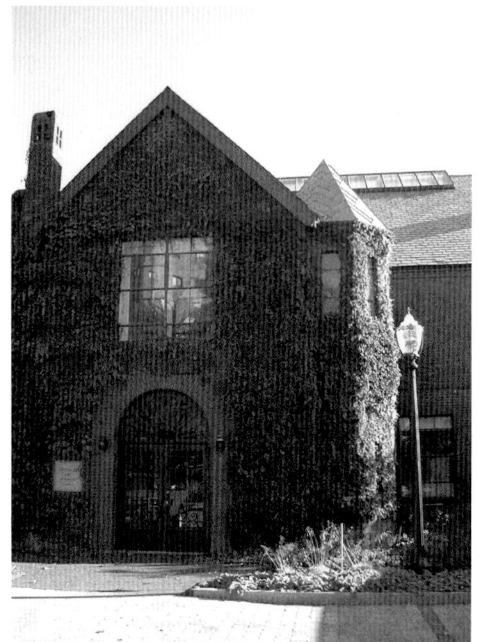

The Fitchburg Art Museum was founded in 1925 through the benevolence of Eleanor Norcross (1854–1923), a Fitchburg artist who lived and painted during the last forty years of her life in Paris, France. Impressed by the many excellent rural museums of that country, Miss Norcross conceived the idea of founding in her native Fitchburg a museum to inspire in people, especially youth, the "joy and inspiration" of art. The bequest of her extensive collections of European paintings, decorative arts, and classical antiquities, along with $10,000 (later matched by area residents), enabled the museum to open in 1929.

During the ensuing years the museum's collections have grown to some 5,000 objects, and its programs have multiplied. In 1989, the Fitchburg Art Museum expanded from its original 10,000-square-foot facility to 40,000 square feet, becoming a block-long complex and the region's most important center for art study and appreciation.

Today, the museum presents twelve changing exhibitions annually, twenty-seven studio classes weekly, and a lively program of lectures, gallery talks, seminars, workshops, demonstrations, recitals, performances, and other activities. The Art Exchange Program offers to business and organization offices rotating exhibitions of fine art posters from more than fifty museums and galleries throughout the world.

In 1995, the Fitchburg Art Museum, in collaboration with the Fitchburg public schools, created a unique school in which all subjects in the state-mandated curriculum are taught in the museum's galleries through the study of collection objects and the pursuit of other art activities. Dedicated in 2000 as the Museum Partnership School, the museum school serves students in grades five through eight, has plans for a high school in process, and helps the museum fulfill its founder's dream by defining itself as a "museum with a school at its heart."

The museum is located in north-central Massachusetts in downtown Fitchburg, close to Route 2 and Interstate 190. Fully accredited and handicapped accessible, the museum is open on a year-round schedule.

FLORENCE GRISWOLD MUSEUM

96 Lyme Street
Old Lyme, Connecticut 06371
860–434–5542
http://www.flogris.org

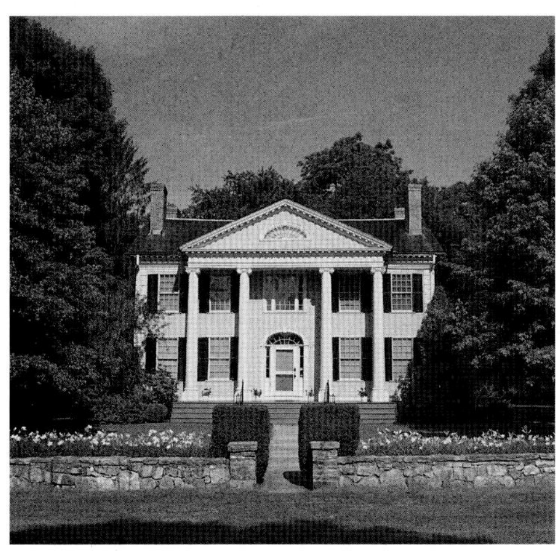

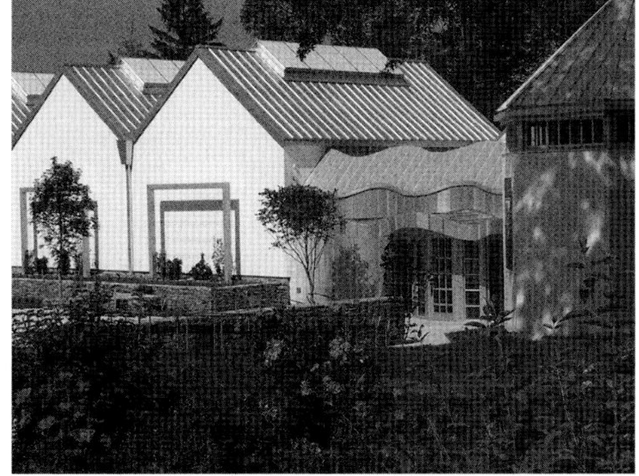

Founded in 1936, the Florence Griswold Museum is a professionally staffed art and history museum that is accredited by the American Association of Museums (AAM). Located in a stately Late Georgian mansion designed by Samuel Belcher and built in 1817, the museum and its grounds served in the early years of the twentieth century as the center for one of America's most famous art colonies. Scores of American Impressionists and Barbizon-influenced painters, often fresh from their studies in France, came to Old Lyme to paint landscapes of the rural countryside. Miss Florence Griswold transformed her family home into the colony's boardinghouse. She converted barns and outbuildings into studios for such nationally prominent artists as Childe Hassam, Willard Leroy Metcalf, and Henry Ward Ranger and provided a congenial environment where, as one artist put it, "every day is so in line with work." Grateful for her hospitality, these and other artists painted on the walls and doors of the house. This unique collection is preserved within the Florence Griswold House today, making the building itself one of the most important aspects of the collection.

Shortly before Florence Griswold's death in 1937, artists, friends, and relatives formed the Florence Griswold Association in order to preserve the house as an art museum. The Florence Griswold House opened to the public in 1947. The museum was first accredited by the AAM in 1978 and designated a national historic landmark in 1993.

With support from the community and beyond, much of the museum's activity in the 1990s focused on reacquiring significant portions of the original Griswold estate with an eye to developing a new kind of museum, one that would encompass art, history, and nature in a New England village setting. Between 1991 and 1997, the museum property grew from two to eleven acres, culminating in 1997 with the purchase of five acres of riverfront property that represents one of the most significant painting grounds of the American Impressionists. For the first time, the museum's campus included the site of the original gardens, outbuildings, and studios of the Lyme art colony.

Over the past five years the Florence Griswold Museum has implemented an ambitious master plan highlighted by the addition of the Hartman Education Center, a dynamic space for hands-on educational activities. In July 2002, the museum opened the Robert and Nancy Krieble Gallery, a modern exhibition gallery and collection storage facility overlooking the Lieutenant River. Designed by Centerbrook Architects, this new center for American art houses the museum's collections, including the renowned Hartford Steam Boiler Collection, which focuses on Connecticut's contribution to our nation's art (figures 46, 47, 48). The museum is currently involved in the restoration and refurnishing of the landmark Florence Griswold House as a boardinghouse for artists, circa 1910. Known today as the Home of American Impressionism, the museum is one of the only places where one can walk through a landscape setting, view paintings of those landscapes, and experience firsthand where a prominent American art colony once lived and worked.

The museum is handicapped accessible and open year-round.

46

WILSON HENRY IRVINE (1869–1936)

Monhegan Bay, Maine, c. 1914

Oil on canvas, 35 × 39"

Florence Griswold Museum

Gift of Mr. and Mrs. George M. Yeager in Honor of the Centennial

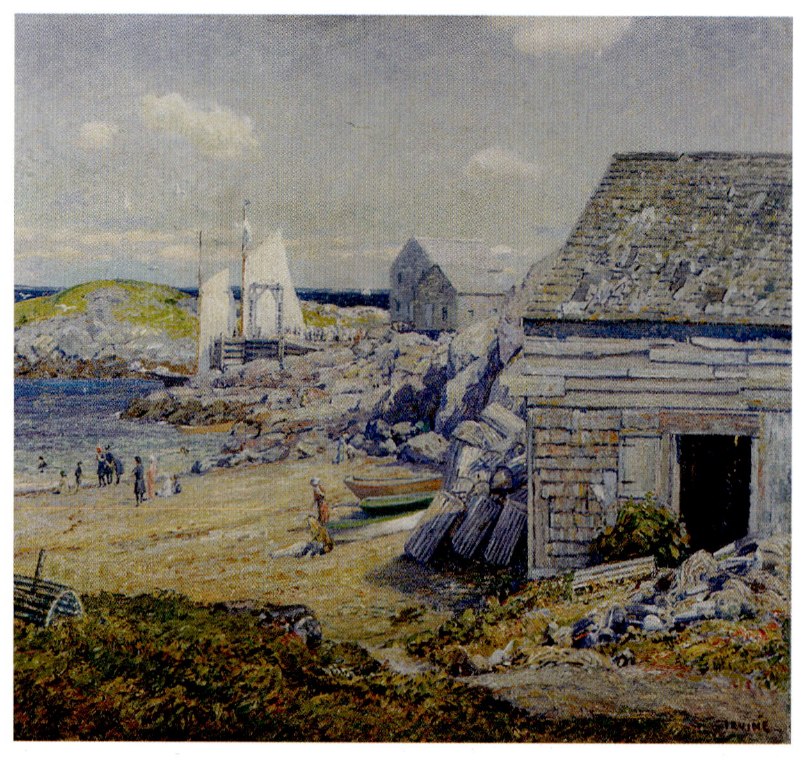

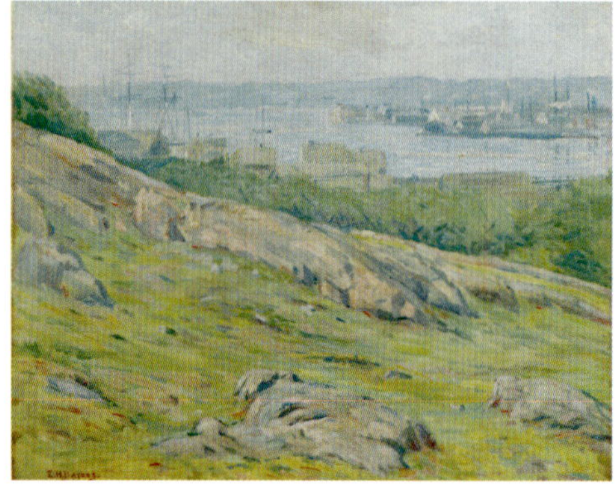

47

ERNEST BARNES (1873–1955)

Mystic Harbor, Connecticut, n.d.

Oil on canvas, 24 × 30"

Florence Griswold Museum

Gift of The Hartford Steam Boiler Inspection and Insurance Company

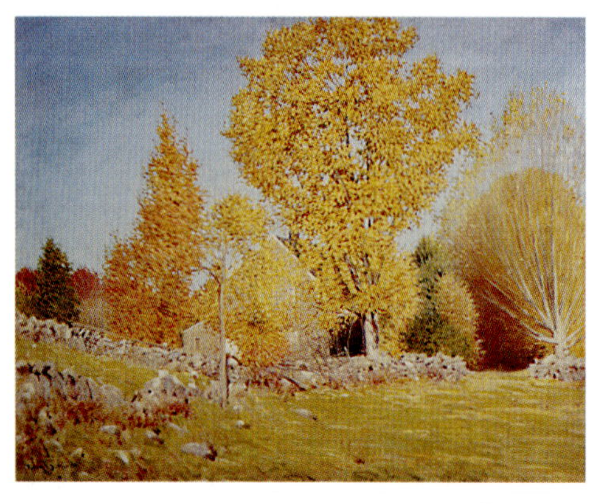

48

FRANK VINCENT DUMOND (1865–1951)

Grassy Hill, 1933

Oil on canvas, 30½ × 24½"

Florence Griswold Museum

Gift of Mrs. Elisabeth DuMond Perry

FRUITLANDS MUSEUMS

102 Prospect Hill Road
Harvard, Massachusetts 01451
978–456–3924
http://www.fruitlands.org

For picturesque beauty both in the near and the distant landscape, the spot has few rivals.
—Bronson Alcott and Charles Lane in the *Dial*, July 1843

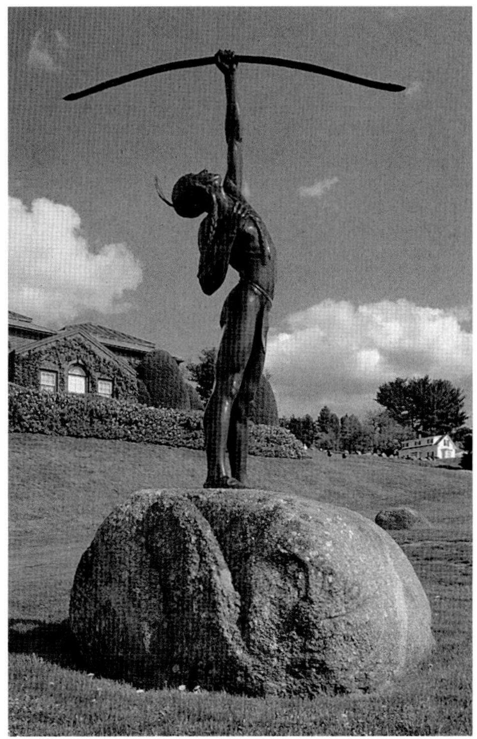

In the small town of Harvard, just thirty miles west of Boston, is one of New England's most unusual and most beautifully sited museums. Fruitlands' pastoral 210-acre campus of fields, wetlands, and woodlands offers views of Mount Wachusett to the west and Mount Monadnock to the north.

The site is named for Fruitlands—the farmhouse of Bronson Alcott's 1843 utopian experiment. The museum was created by Clara Endicott Sears after she renovated the farmhouse in 1914, opening it to the public as a museum of the transcendental utopian movement. Over the next thirty years the site grew to include Native American art and artifacts, a Shaker collection, and a picture gallery of American primitive portraits and Hudson River School landscapes, including those by Albert Bierstadt and Frederic E. Church. Recently the museum's mission has broadened to celebrate the spirit and history of New England's people and their relationship to the land.

Fruitlands is one of those rare and inspirational places that offers a retreat from worldly pressures, an opportunity to consider the idealism of an earlier age, and a chance to explore the past and imagine the future. Fruitlands uses its rich collections to reveal the meaning and purpose, choices and decisions of the generations of people who have inhabited the "Valley of the Nashaway." These inhabitants include the Native people, colonial farmers, nineteenth-century utopians, Shakers, artists, and others whose identity, aspirations, values, and spirit were rooted in New England.

The education staff at Fruitlands Museums is committed to raising awareness of, and expanding access to, its collections by continuing to develop programs that serve a variety of audiences. School programs include Paths to the Past tours, outreach programs, and an online learning component of the Web site. Temporary exhibitions and a full schedule of special events and activities offer visitors many options for exploring the museum's art, history, and landscape.

Fruitlands' collections, trails, museum shop, and Tea Room are open mid-May through mid-October.

FULLER MUSEUM OF ART

455 Oak Street

Brockton, Massachusetts 02301

508–588–6000

http://www.fullermuseum.org

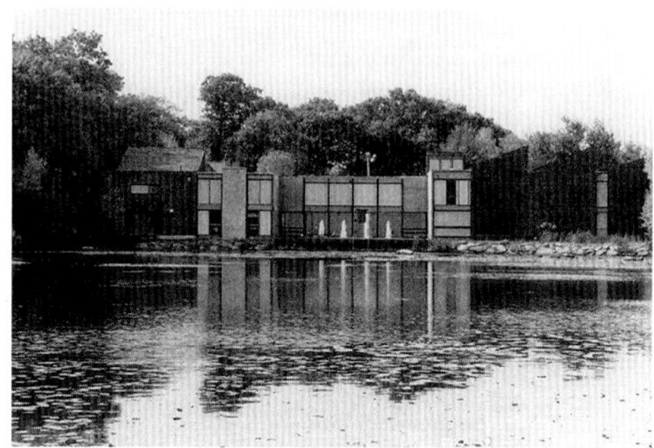

The Fuller Museum of Art was founded in 1969 as the Brockton Art Center/Fuller Memorial with funds provided by the bequest of Myron L. Fuller, a Brockton geologist and entrepreneur. Since its inception, the institution has been dedicated to the arts and art education. Although not originally conceived as a collecting institution, the art center began receiving gifts of art almost immediately. In 1976 the American Association of Museums granted accreditation, which was renewed in 1995. On its twentieth anniversary, the museum's formal name was changed to the Fuller Museum of Art, honoring its original benefactor and acknowledging its regional scope. Currently, the museum consists of 21,000 square feet of space, including galleries, an auditorium, classrooms/studios, a conservation laboratory, and storage rooms.

In the years since the founding of the FMA, the Brockton community has changed dramatically, experiencing shifts in demographics and a decline in economic activity. The Fuller has continuously risen to the challenge of meeting the evolving needs of its audience. The result is that the Fuller Museum of Art has emerged as the largest visual arts institution and resource for arts education in southeastern Massachusetts.

In 2002, the board of directors of the Fuller Museum of Art voted unanimously to change the focus of the institution to the field of contemporary craft. Contemporary craft includes one-of-a-kind works of art in a variety of media (glass, metal, wood, ceramics, fiber) with a basis in both form and function. The Fuller is now among the ranks of a select few craft museums in the United States, including the American Museum of Arts and Design (formerly the American Craft Museum), the Renwick Gallery of the Smithsonian, the Corning Museum of Glass, the Mint Museum of Art + Design, and the Racine Art Museum. Future programming will showcase master craftspeople as well as emerging contemporary artists who use craft materials in new ways. The New England region has a rich history of crafts and workmanship, and the museum collaborates with craft institutions, recognized craft artists, galleries, community associations, and patrons to heighten public awareness, understanding, and appreciation of fine crafts.

In addition to changing exhibitions, a gallery remains dedicated to exhibitions of the permanent collection, which contains the work of many well-known artists. The museum presents a full schedule of programs, lectures, special events, and docent-led tours. School programs and Art ASPIRE, an outreach afterschool program in which professional artists travel to schools, extend the opportunities of art appreciation and instruction for younger audiences. Classes and workshops for children and adults include topics ranging from drawing and painting, to working with clay and glassblowing.

Situated on twenty-two acres of woodland in Brockton, on the shores of Upper Porter's Pond, adjacent to D.W. Field Park (inspired by Frederick Law Olmsted), the museum is housed in an award-winning, accessible, contemporary building designed by J. Timothy Anderson. It is just south of Boston, close to the major highways, and is open year-round.

LYMAN ALLYN ART MUSEUM

625 Williams Street
New London, Connecticut 06320
860–443–2545
http://www.lymanallyn.org

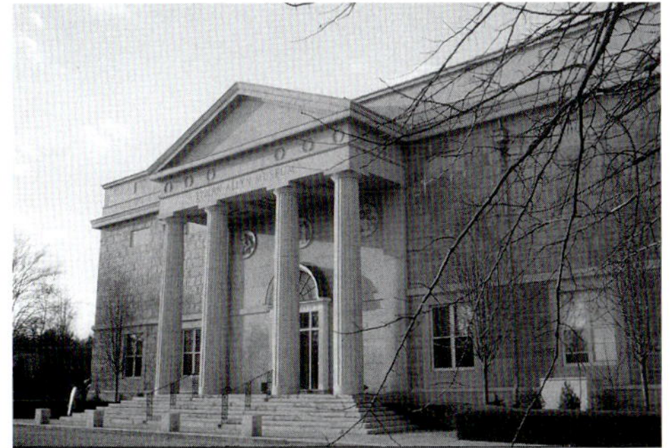

Envisioned as a place that would meld the very best that small and large museums have to offer, the Lyman Allyn Art Museum gives visitors an opportunity to view a first-rate collection, as well as enjoy and learn about art and culture. The museum was founded in 1926 by Harriet Allyn as a memorial to her father, Captain Lyman Allyn, who rose from sailor to sea captain to fleet owner. Among the values Captain Allyn instilled in his children were industriousness, a keen sense of business, and generosity to the community. His youngest child, Harriet, deemed a fine arts museum to be a fitting tribute and opportunity to contribute to the life of the New London community. Thanks to the efforts of Arthur Day and Clement Scott, two respected bankers and authorities on the fine arts, the museum opened in 1932 with Winslow Ames as its first director.

Ames, known as a "live wire," worked to acquire and purchase numerous objects for the museum, including its largest gift, the bequest of Virginia Palmer. The museum now boasts an impressive collection of more than 30,000 objects. These holdings include contemporary, modern, and early American fine arts, American Impressionist paintings, and decorative arts of Connecticut. Paintings by William T. Gooding and William L. Richardson, among others, celebrate the sea, which played such an important role in Captain Allyn's life and continues to influence the lives of New London inhabitants.

The museum is housed in a handsome neoclassical building designed by Charles A. Platt, architect of the Freer Gallery of Art in Washington, D.C.

The Lyman Allyn Art Museum offers a year-round schedule of changing exhibitions. Selections from the permanent collections are on view (figure 49), together with a variety of special exhibitions featuring artists and topics of contemporary interest. Programs including lectures, concerts, dance performances, workshops, films, and "closer look" tours continue to make the museum a lively and exciting place to visit. Located on the grounds, the Children's Art Park is *always* open, year-round and in any weather!

The museum, which is handicapped accessible, is open year-round.

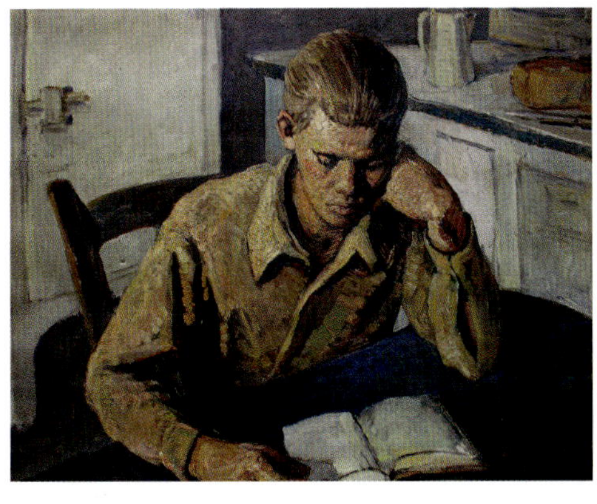

49
RUSSELL CHENEY (1881–1945)
Fred Reading, n.d. (20th c.)
Oil on canvas, 31 × 34"
Lyman Allyn Art Museum

MATTATUCK MUSEUM

144 West Main Street
Waterbury, Connecticut 06702
203–753–0381
http://www.MattatuckMuseum.org

The Mattatuck Museum is a beacon of culture in the center of Waterbury, Connecticut. Within its exhibits, spacious galleries, restaurant, 300-seat performing arts center, research library, classrooms, and outdoor courtyard, tens of thousands of people enjoy special programs, exhibits on art and history, music, theater, fine dining, great parties, and a multitude of other cultural and educational activities every year.

The museum traces its roots to the Mattatuck Historical Society, founded in 1877 and incorporated in 1902. In 1985, the renowned architect Cesar Pelli designed renovations and additions to the 1912 building, a former Masonic temple that today houses the Mattatuck Museum.

Spacious and classically detailed art galleries display the museum's collections of work by American masters associated with the state of Connecticut. In its survey of three centuries, the collection includes eighteenth-, nineteenth-, and twentieth-century works by artists such as John Trumbull, Frederic E. Church, George Inness, John Frederick Kensett, Maurice Prendergast, Everett Shinn, Josef Albers, Yves Tanguy, Alexander Calder, and Arshile Gorky. Changing exhibits showcase contemporary artists and Connecticut artists of the past, and highlight aspects of the region's history (figures 50, 51). The museum's Fine Art collection has been digitized and made accessible to the public both online and at the museum, through interactive kiosks, and through computer terminals available for art researchers in the Thaler Cohen Study Center.

Brass Roots is an extensive and permanent history exhibit of striking contemporary design, giving museum visitors dramatic you-were-there experiences of the unfolding of the region's history. From early tools, finely crafted eighteenth-century furniture, wooden-works clocks, factory machinery, early cameras, Art Deco tableware, Charles Goodyear's rubber desk, and a display of other local products, *Brass Roots* winds its way through time, offering the viewer glimpses of life and times long past. The exhibit focuses on the social history of western Connecticut and particularly the Naugatuck Valley, the nation's leading producer of brass and brass products in the nineteenth century. The exhibit is organized around the themes of work, family life, and community institutions, presenting the stories of the brass industry and the people who came to this region over the last 175 years to work in the brass industry. The exhibit features the experiences of workers, women, and immigrants, along with the stories of inventors and entrepreneurs, in displays that include audio components with immigrants' and brass workers' stories and re-creations of a factory and a boardinghouse. In addition, the third floor of the museum houses The Waterbury Button Museum, featuring 10,000 buttons made in Waterbury and around the world.

The fully accredited Mattatuck Museum is conveniently located on Waterbury Green, accessible from either Interstate 84 or Route 8. Secure, well-lighted parking is available on Park Place, at the top of the street behind the museum. The museum is open year-round and is wheelchair accessible.

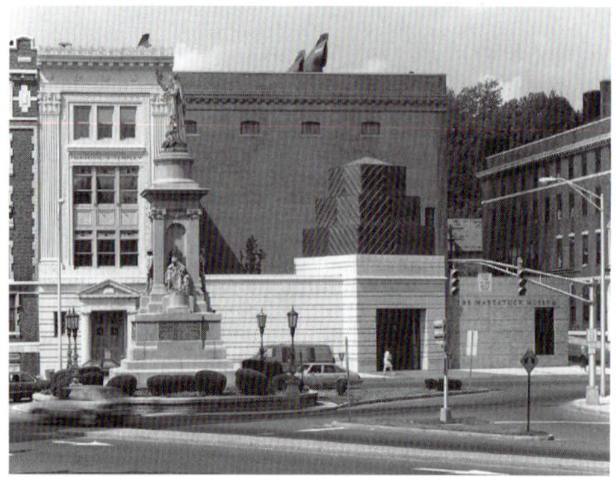

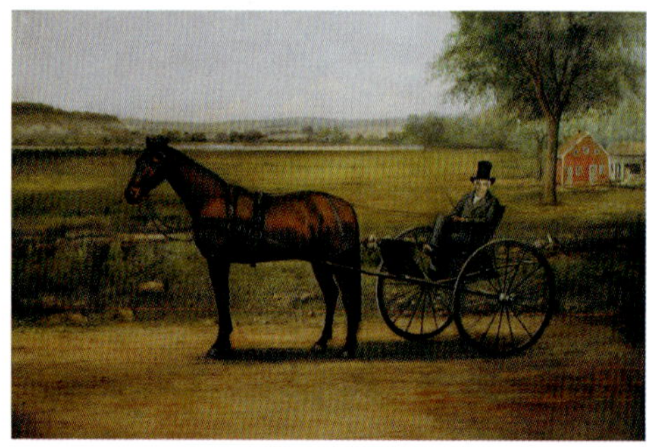

50
UNKNOWN
Portrait of Dr. Samuel Elton and His Riding Chair, c. 1850
Oil on canvas, 26 × 38"
Collection of Mattatuck Museum, Waterbury, CT

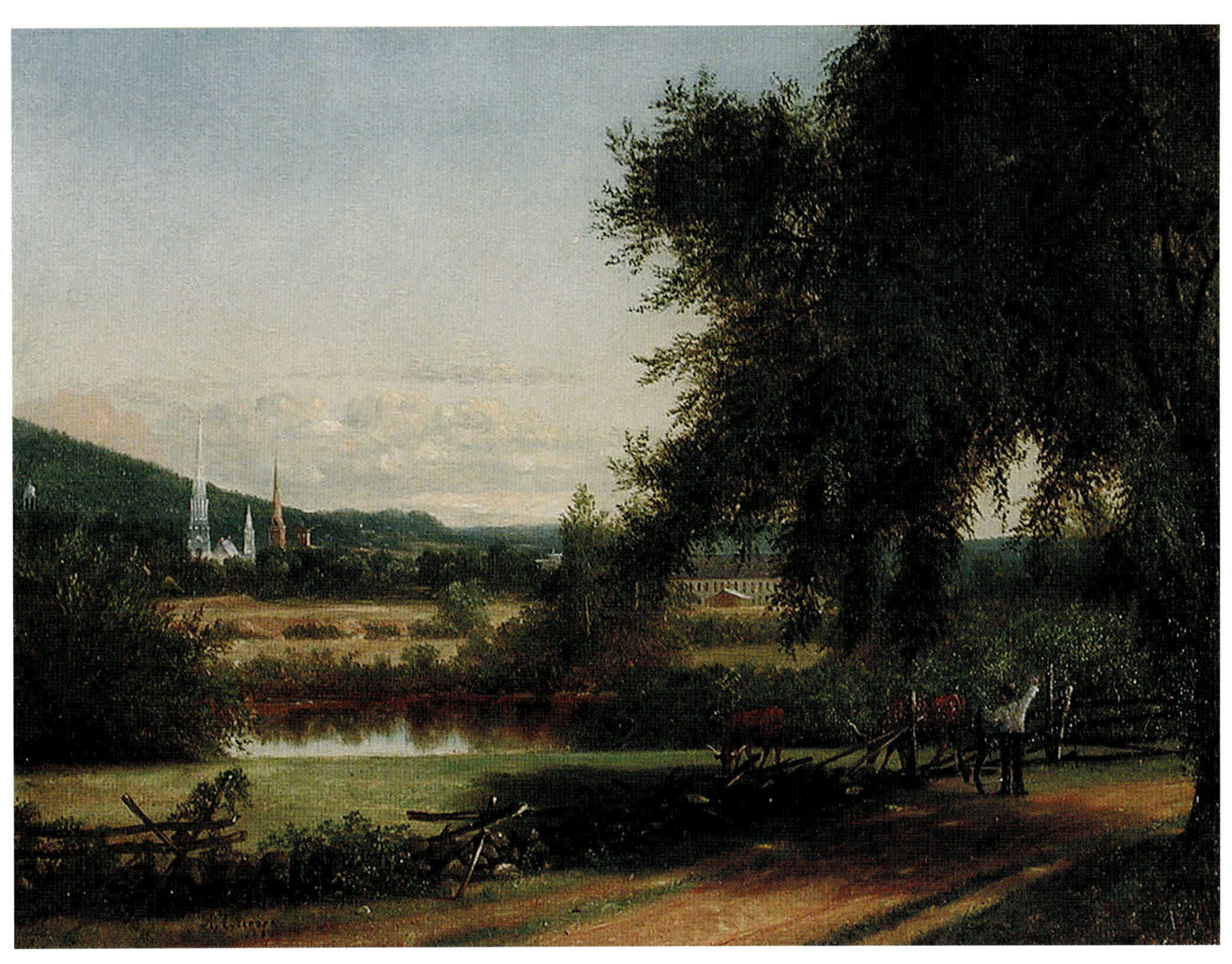

51
NELSON AUGUSTUS MOORE (1824–1902)
Church Spires in Waterbury, 1864
Oil on canvas, 15 × 21½"
Collection of Mattatuck Museum, Waterbury, CT

NEW BRITAIN MUSEUM OF AMERICAN ART

56 Lexington Street
New Britain, Connecticut 06052
860–229–0257
http://www.nbmaa.org

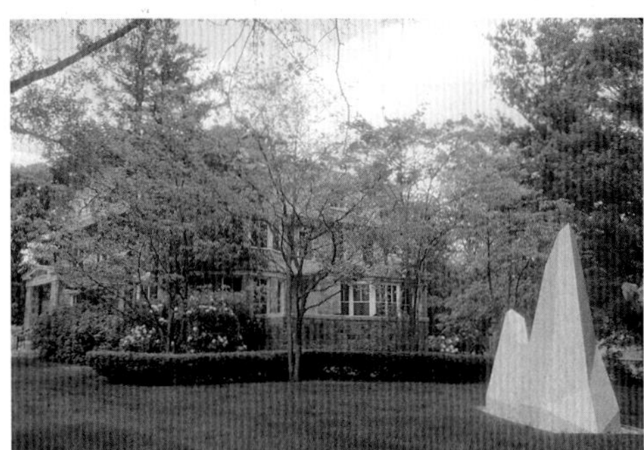

"Three centuries of great American art in one incredible collection." That phrase defines the New Britain Museum of American Art, which celebrated its one-hundredth anniversary in 2003 marking a century of exciting growth. Attracting some 50,000 visitors every year, the museum is a cultural gem located next to Frederick Law Olmsted's historic Walnut Hill Park. Occupying a turn-of-the-century mansion since 1937, the New Britain Museum of American Art traces its beginnings to 1903, when private citizens began a public art collection for the enjoyment and education of the public. Early on, the museum leadership embraced the idea that the collection would focus exclusively on American art, so that today, the museum collection numbers nearly 5,000 oils, watercolors, drawings, graphics, and works of sculpture housed in nineteen galleries.

The visitor can experience an entire survey of our nation's art history, from John Singleton Copley, Frederic Edwin Church, Thomas Cole, Georgia O'Keeffe, and the complex Thomas Hart Benton murals *Arts of Life in America*, to New Britian native Sol LeWitt, to name a few. The collection is especially rich in American Impressionism. Mary Cassatt, William Merritt Chase, Theodore Robinson, Childe Hassam, John Henry Twachtman, Julian Alden Weir, Willard Leroy Metcalf, Frank Weston Benson, Frederick Frieseke, Richard Miller, Arthur Clifton Goodwin, Ernest Lawson, Maurice Prendergast, and Guy Wiggins are all well represented. Because only 2 percent of the collection can be shown at any one time, objects on display are constantly changed.

The Sanford B. D. Low Memorial Illustration Collection, begun in 1962, comprises more than 1,400 works, including works by Newell Convers Wyeth, Howard Pyle, and Norman Rockwell (figure 52). The Low Illustration Collection is the nation's first museum-based collection covering the history of American illustration from the nineteenth century to the present.

Beyond its extensive permanent collection, the museum offers several major visiting exhibitions every year and presents the work of cutting-edge contemporary artists in the very popular NEW/NOW gallery.

First Fridays every month at the museum offer live music, refreshments, and camaraderie from 5:30 until 8:00 P.M. The museum also sponsors a highly successful arts and crafts festival every year, attracting thousands of people to its Walnut Hill Park location. Drawing families with children and schoolchildren into the institution are ongoing educational programs that provide hands-on arts experiences. Minority outreach programs extend beyond the walls of the museum into the community, making the arts more accessible to all residents of the region. Fully accredited and wheelchair accessible, the New Britain Museum is open year-round.

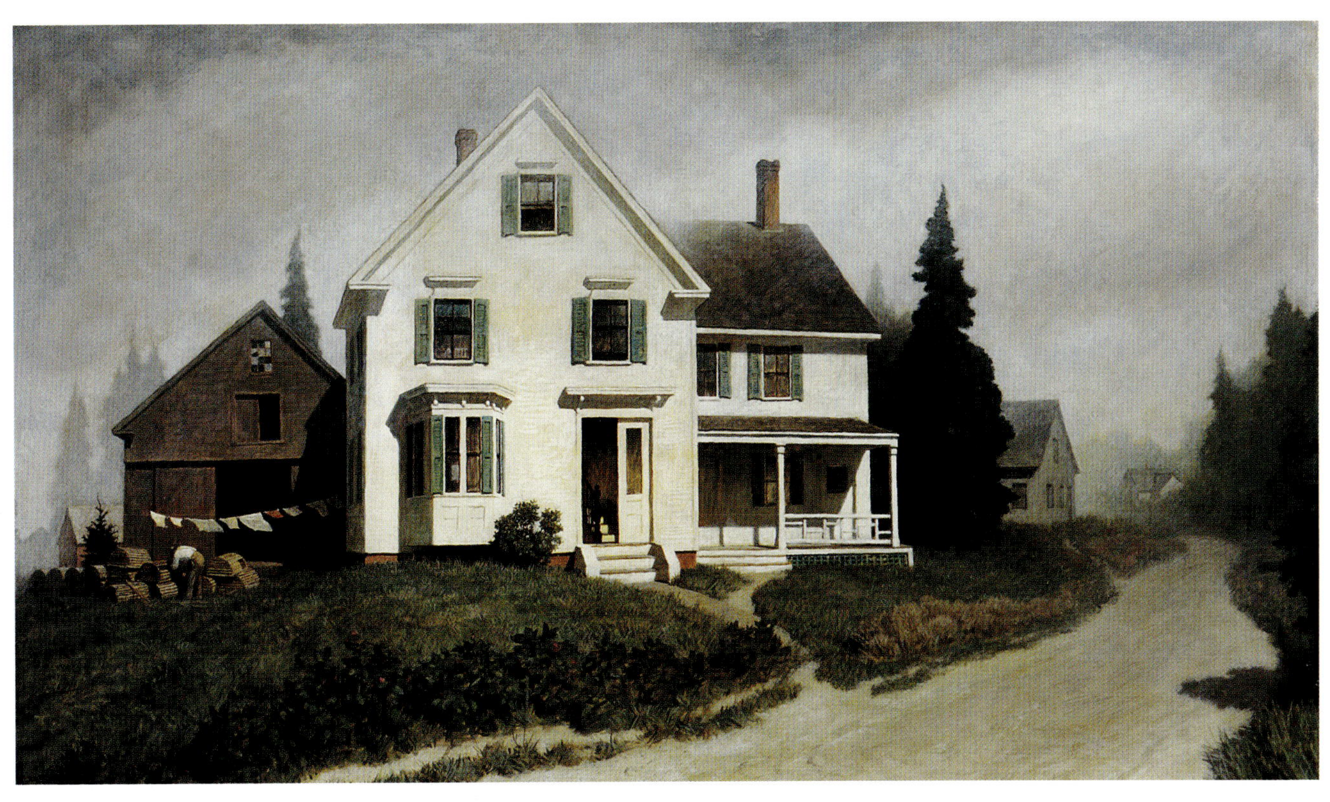

52

NEWELL CONVERS WYETH (1882–1945)

Mrs. Cushman's House, 1944

Egg tempera on board, 21½ × 37⅜"

Harriet Russell Stanley Fund

Collection of the New Britain Museum of American Art

NEWPORT ART MUSEUM AND ART ASSOCIATION

76 Bellevue Avenue
Newport, Rhode Island 02840
401–848–8200
http://www.newportartmuseum.com

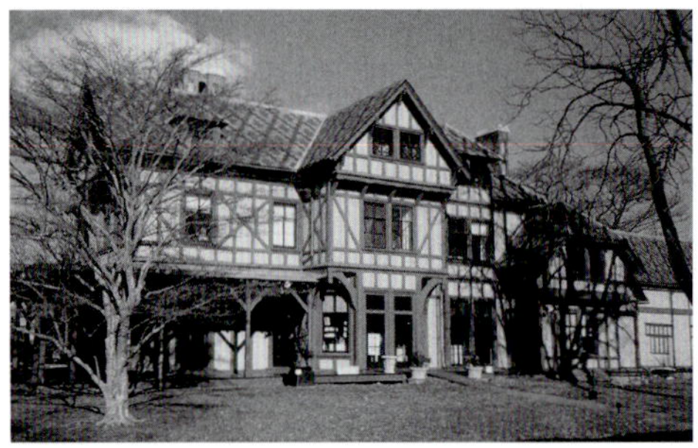

The Newport Art Museum and Art Association is a repository of cultural history, a leading center for emerging and established artists in southeastern New England, and a vibrant community resource.

The Newport Art Museum has deep historical ties to the region, its roots extending back to 1912, when the Art Association of Newport was founded by a group of important American artists and community leaders including social activist and Pulitzer prizewinning author Maud Howe Elliott, Helena and Louisa Sturtevant, and William Sergeant Kendall. The focal point of the organization's three-building campus is even older: the architecturally significant John N. A. Griswold House was completed in 1864. Griswold House was designed by Richard Morris Hunt and was the prototype for the mature Stick style of American architecture. The Art Association was never intended to be an exclusive art club for professional artists and wealthy patrons: it was dedicated to promoting and encouraging art education among all members of the community. The inclusive nature of the organization made it unique in its time and helped to ensure its survival into the twenty-first century. The Newport Art Museum is the nation's oldest continuously operating public art association. Griswold House is a national historic landmark and an official project of Save America's Treasures.

Today, the Newport Art Museum and Art Association thrives as an integral part of the community. The museum's collection focuses on the visual arts of southeastern New England with an emphasis on the Newport area. Exhibitions reflect both the lively art scene of the present and the rich heritage of the past (figure 53). The museum's school, the Coleman Center for Creative Studies, is a vigorous center for art education, offering classes, camps, workshops, and outreach programs to people of all ages, backgrounds, and artistic abilities. Newport Art Museum facilitates community connections by hosting a wide variety of cultural and social events throughout the year including a winter lecture series, music concerts, family events, galas, and arts festivals. After almost a century of activity, the organization's aims remain remarkably constant: to provide a center for learning, creating, and connection within the heart of a diverse community. The handicapped-accessible museum is open year-round, and group tours may be arranged.

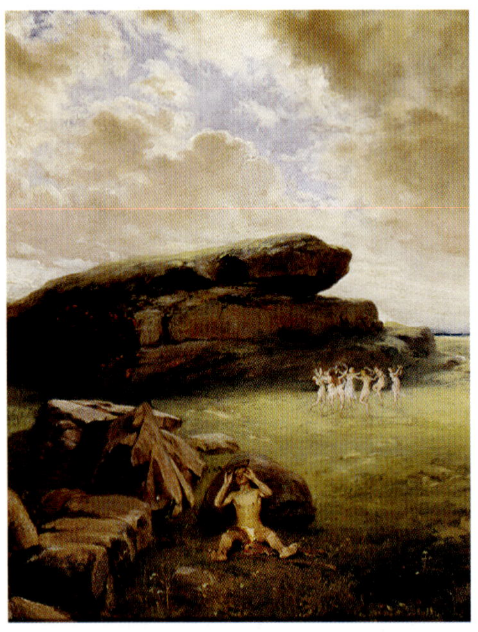

53
IGNAZ GAUGENGIGL (1855–1932)
The Idyll: Bishop Berkeley's Rock, c. 1885
Oil on panel, 11 × 9"
Collection of the Newport Art Museum and Art Association
Gift of Mr. and Mrs. William Vareika

PROVINCETOWN ART ASSOCIATION AND MUSEUM

460 Commercial Street
Provincetown, Massachusetts 02657
508–487–1750
http://www.paam.org

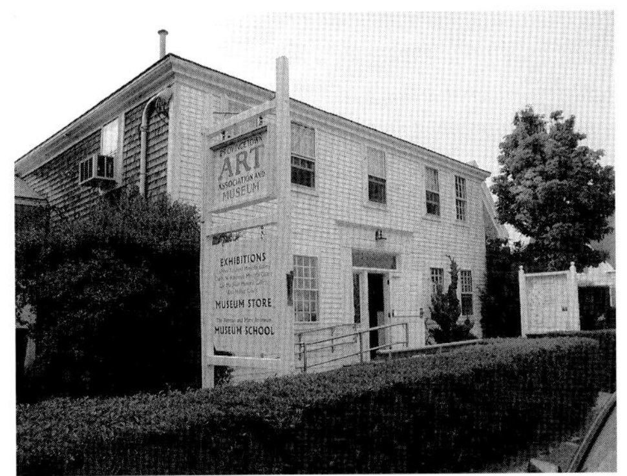

The Provincetown art colony originated in 1899 with the founding of the Cape Cod School of Art. It continues to attract artists and art enthusiasts to a remarkable venue where clear light and natural landscape abound.

The Provincetown Art Association and Museum dates to 1914, when a group of artists and townspeople responded to the need for an established arts institution. The collection began with donations from five major painters of the time: Charles Webster Hawthorne, William Halsall, Gerrit Beneker, Oscar Gieberich, and E. Ambrose Webster. The holdings, now nearly 2,000 works of art, represent almost six hundred artists who have worked, at one time or another, on the Outer Cape since 1900.

The Provincetown Art Association and Museum is notable in that it serves as both a collecting institution and a professional artists' association. Its collection is an incredible resource that reflects the various movements within the art world. Artists represented include Milton Avery, Edwin Dickinson, Red Grooms, Wolf Kahn, Franz Kline, George McNeil, Ross Moffett, Robert Motherwell, Man Ray, and Andy Warhol.

The collections are a record of the changing art movements and important historical events that have marked American history during the last century. The Provincetown art colony played a significant role in the history of American art, both welcoming and resisting art movements. Less than twelve years into its existence, the association experienced an acute division between champions of traditional and abstract art. In 1927 the Art Association addressed this split by holding a separate modernist show each year. This power struggle lasted ten years or more before the division lines became indistinguishable.

One of Provincetown's most affluent painters, Hans Hofmann, opened his school of painting in 1934. His unique method of instruction focused on Abstract Expressionism and Cubism. The 1930s through the 1950s produced a cultural upheaval. The Hofmann School and the influx of artists from Europe brought art in Provincetown to a new level. Several Hofmann students, including Robert Henry, Lillian Orlowsky, Paul Resika, and Tony Vevers, currently work and live in Provincetown.

The Provincetown Print, a conventional American white-line woodcut, was developed by a core group of six American artists influenced by Japanese woodcuts and color lithography in Europe in the 1890s. Four of these, Ada Gilmore, Ethel Mars, Mildred McMillen, and Maud Squire, arrived in Provincetown in 1915. Together with Juliette Nichols and B. J. O. Nordfeldt, they formed the Provincetown Printmakers. After nearly eighty-seven years of Provincetown printmaking, contemporary printmakers such as Kathryn Smith and William Evaul carry on the tradition.

Through changing exhibitions, member shows, a museum school, its research archives, and a rich variety of programs, the Provincetown Art Association and Museum "promotes and cultivates the practice and appreciation of all branches of the fine arts."

The accessible museum is open throughout the year on a variable schedule.

❦ Notes

Grinnell, *Founding Visions* (pages 1–13)

1. Newport Art Museum Archives.

2. American Association of Museums, *Excellence and Equity: Education and the Public Dimension of Museums* (Washington, D.C.: American Association of Museums, 1992), 7.

Becker, *the American Artist in New England* (pages 19–43)

1. For a thoughtful study of American artists and their interest in New England subject matter during this period see William H. Truettner and Roger B. Stein, eds., *Picturing Old New England: Image and Memory* (Washington, D.C.: Smithsonian Museum of American Art, 1999).

2. See Katherine H. Campbell, "Albert Bierstadt and the White Mountains," *Archives of American Art Journal* 21, no. 3 (1981): 14–23; and Nancy K. Anderson and Linda S. Ferber, *Albert Bierstadt: Art and Enterprise* (New York: Hudson Hills Press in association with the Brooklyn Museum, 1991).

3. See Nicolai Cikovsky, Jr., *George Inness* (New York: Harry N. Abrams, 1993); and Cikovsky and Michael Quick, *George Inness* (Los Angeles: Los Angeles County Museum of Art, 1985).

4. See Theresa A Carbone and Patricia Hills, *Eastman Johnson: Painting America* (New York: Rizzoli, 1999); Patricia Hills, *The Genre Painting of Eastman Johnson* (New York: Garland Publishing Company, 1977; and Elizabeth Johns, *American Genre Painting: The Politics of Everyday Life* (New Haven, Conn.: Yale University Press, 1991).

5. For a closer examination of this painting and *Camden Mountains from the South Entrance to the Harbor* see Pamela J. Belanger, *Maine in America: American Art at the Farnsworth Art Museum* (Rockland, Maine: Farnsworth Art Museum, 2000), 56. For a survey of marine painting see John Wilmerding, *American Marine Painting* (New York: Harry N. Abrams, 1987). For extended treatment on Lane's paintings see John Wilmerding, *Paintings of Fitz Hugh Lane* (Washington D.C.: National Gallery of Art, 1988).

6. See Linda S. Ferber, *William Trost Richards: American Landscape and Marine Painter, 1833–1905* (Brooklyn: The Brooklyn Museum, 1973).

7. See Theordore E. Stebbins, Jr., *The Life and Work of Martin Johnson Heade: A Critical Analysis and Catalogue Raisonné* (New Haven, Conn.: Yale University Press, 2000); and Stebbins, *Martin Johnson Heade* (Boston: Museum of Fine Arts, 1999).

8. See Warren Adelson, Jay E. Cantor, and William H. Gerdts, *Childe Hassam: Cosmopolitan and Patriot* (New York: Abbeville Press, 1999); Kathleen M. Burnside, *Childe Hassam in Connecticut* (Old Lyme, Conn.: Lyme Historical Society, 1987); and Ulrich W. Hiesinger, *Childe Hassam: American Impressionist* (New York: Prestel Verlag, 1999).

9. For a survey of art colonies and American Impressionism see William H. Gerdts, *American Impressionism* (New York: Abbeville Press, 1984).

10. See Jack Becker, *Henry Ward Ranger and the Humanized Landscape* (Old Lyme, Conn.: Lyme Historical Society, 1999).

11. On the development of the Lyme art colony see Jeffrey W. Andersen, "A Season in Lyme: Life among the Artists," in *En Plein Air: The Art Colonies of East Hampton and Old Lyme, 1880–1930* (East Hampton, N.Y.: Guild Hall of East Hampton, 1989).

12. See the essay by J. Gray Sweeney in Belanger, *Maine in America*, 106.

13. For a full discussion of this painting see the catalogue entry by Jack Becker in Lisa N. Peters and Peter M. Lukehart, eds., *Visions of Home: American Impressionist Images of Suburban Leisure and Country Comfort* (Carlisle, Pa.: Trout Gallery, Dickinson College, 1997), 96. For more on Metcalf see Richard J. Boyle, *Sunlight and Shadow: The Life and Art of Willard L. Metcalf* (New York: Abbeville Press, 1987).

14. For a brief discussion of this work see Jane and Will Curtis and Frank Lieberman, *Monhegan: The Artists' Island* (Camden, Maine: Down East Books, 1995), 169. For more on the artist see Harold Spencer, *Wilson Henry Irvine and the Poetry of Light* (Old Lyme, Conn.: Lyme Historical Society, 1998).

15. For a broader examination of New England during this period see the following: Alan Axelrod, ed., *The Colonial Revival in America* (New York: Henry Francis du Pont Winterthur Museum, 1985); Dona Brown, *Inventing New England: Regional Tourism in the Nineteenth Century* (Washington, D.C.: Smithsonian Institution Press, 1995); David Glassberg, *American Historical Pageantry: The Uses of Tradition in the Early Twentieth Century* (Chapel Hill: University of North Carolina Press, 1990); Eric Hobsbawm and Terence Ranger,

eds., *The Invention of Tradition* (New York: Cambridge University Press, 1983); John Brinckerhoff Jackson, *The Necessity for Ruins* (Amherst: University of Massachusetts Press, 1980); Michael Kammen, *Mystic Chords of Memory: The Transformation of Tradition in American Culture* (New York: Knopf, 1991); T. J. Jackson Lears, *No Place of Grace: Antimodernism and the Transformation of American Culture, 1880–1920* (New York: Pantheon Books, 1981); James Lindgren, *Preserving Historic New England: Preservation, Progressivism, and the Remaking of Memory* (New York: Oxford University Press, 1995); and Kathleen Pyne, *Art and the Higher Life: Painting and Evolutionary Thought in Late Nineteenth-Century America* (Austin: University of Texas Press, 1996).

16. For a complete discussion of Bellows see Michael Quick et al., *The Paintings of George Bellows* (New York: Harry N. Abrams, 1992). See also Marianne Doezema, *George Bellows and Urban America* (New Haven, Conn.: Yale University Press, 1992).

17. For more detailed discussion of Marin see Sheldon Reich, *John Marin: A Stylistic Analysis and Catalogue Raisonné* (Tucson: University of Arizona Press, 1970). See also Ruth E. Fine, *John Marin* (Washington, D.C.: National Gallery of Art; New York: Abbeville Press, 1990). For Stieglitz circle see Marcia Brennan, *Painting Gender, Constructing Theory: The Alfred Stieglitz Circle and American Formalist Aesthetics* (Cambridge, Mass.: The MIT Press, 2001).

18. See Jane Kallir, *The Artist behind the Myth* (New York: Clarkson Potter for Galerie St. Etienne, 1982), and Kallir, *The World of Grandma Moses* (Washington, D.C.: The International Exhibitions Foundation, 1984).

19. See Walter Licht, *Industrializing America: The Nineteenth Century* (Baltimore: Johns Hopkins University Press, 1995); Alice Marie O'Mara Piron, "Urban Metaphor in American Art and Literature, 1910–1930," Ph.D. diss., Northwestern University, Evanston, Ill., 1982; and Dominic Ricciotti, "The Urban Scene: Images of the City in American Painting, 1890–1930," Ph.D. diss., Indiana University, Bloomington, 1977.

20. For Edward Hopper see Gail Levin, *Edward Hopper* (New York: Knopf, 1995); and Levin, *Edward Hopper: A Catalogue Raisonné* (New York: Norton, 1995). For Rockwell Kent see Richard V. West, *"An Enkindled Eye": The Paintings of Rockwell Kent* (Santa Barbara, Calif.: Santa Barbara Museum of Art, 1985).

Selected Bibliography

Adelson, Warren, Jay E. Cantor, and William H. Gerdts. *Childe Hassam: Cosmopolitan and Patriot.* New York: Abbeville Press, 1999.

Andersen, Jeffrey W. *The American Artist in Connecticut: The Legacy of the Hartford Steam Boiler Collection.* Old Lyme, Conn.: Florence Griswold Museum, 2002.

———. *Old Lyme: The American Barbizon.* Old Lyme, Conn.: Florence Griswold Museum, 1982.

———. "A Season in Lyme: Life among the Artists." *En Plein Air: The Art Colonies of East Hampton and Old Lyme, 1880–1930.* East Hampton, N.Y.: Guild Hall of East Hampton, 1989.

Anderson, Nancy K., and Linda S. Ferber. *Albert Bierstadt: Art and Enterprise.* New York: Hudson Hills Press in association with the Brooklyn Museum, 1991.

Art Complex Museum. *20th Anniversary Catalogue.* Duxbury, Mass.: Art Complex Museum, 1991.

Axelrod, Alan, ed. *The Colonial Revival in America.* New York: Henry Francis du Pont Winterthur Museum, 1985.

Barton, Cynthia C. *History's Daughter: The Life of Clara Endicott Sears, Founder of Fruitlands Museums.* Harvard, Mass.: Fruitlands Museums, 1998.

Becker, Jack. *Henry Ward Ranger and the Humanized Landscape.* Old Lyme, Conn.: Lyme Historical Society, 1999.

Bedford, Faith Andrews. *Frank W. Benson: American Impressionist.* New York: Rizzoli, 1994.

Belanger, Pamela J. *Inventing Acadia: Artists and Tourists at Mount Desert.* Rockland, Maine: Farnsworth Art Museum, 1999.

———. *Maine in America: American Art at the Farnsworth Art Museum.* Rockland, Maine: Farnsworth Art Museum, 2000.

Bennett, Dean B. *The Forgotten Nature of New England.* Camden, Maine: Down East Books, 1996.

Bercovitch, Sacvan. *The Puritan Origins of the American Self.* New Haven, Conn.: Yale University Press, 1975.

Bermingham, Ann. *Landscape and Ideology.* Berkeley: University of California Press, 1987.

Bermingham, Peter. *American Art in the Barbizon Mood.* Washington, D.C.: Smithsonian Institution Press, 1975.

Boyle, Richard J. *Sunlight and Shadow: The Life and Art of Willard L. Metcalf.* New York: Abbeville Press, 1987.

Brennan, Marcia. *Painting Gender, Constructing Theory: The Alfred Stieglitz Circle and American Formalist Aesthetics.* Cambridge, Mass.: The MIT Press, 2001.

Brown, Dona. *Inventing New England: Regional Tourism in the Nineteenth Century.* Washington, D.C.: Smithsonian Institution Press, 1995.

Buell, Lawrence. *The Environmental Imagination: Thoreau, Nature Writing, and the Formation of American Culture.* Cambridge, Mass.: Belknap Press of Harvard University Press, 1995.

Burke, Doreen Bolger, et al. *In Pursuit of Beauty: Americans and the Aesthetic Movement.* New York: Metropolitan Museum of Art, 1986.

Burns, Sarah. *Inventing the Modern Artist: Art & Culture in Gilded Age America.* New Haven, Conn.: Yale University Press, 1996.

———. *Pastoral Inventions: Rural Life in Nineteenth-Century American Art and Culture.* Philadelphia: Temple University Press, 1989.

Burnside, Kathleen M. *Childe Hassam in Connecticut.* Old Lyme, Conn.: Lyme Historical Society, 1987.

Campbell, Katherine H. "Albert Bierstadt and the White Mountains." *Archives of American Art Journal* 21, no. 3 (1981): 14–23.

Carbone, Theresa A., and Patricia Hills. *Eastman Johnson: Painting America.* New York: Rizzoli, 1999.

Cash, Sarah. *Ominous Hush: The Thunderstorm Paintings of Martin Johnson Heade.* Fort Worth: Amon Carter Museum, 1994.

Chotner, Deborah, Lisa N. Peters, and Kathleen A. Pyne. *John Twachtman: Connecticut Landscapes.* Washington, D.C.: National Gallery of Art, 1989.

Cikovsky, Nicolai, Jr. *George Inness.* New York: Harry N. Abrams, 1993.

———, and Michael Quick. *George Inness.* Los Angeles: Los Angeles County Museum of Art, 1985.

Connecticut and American Impressionism. Storrs: William Benton Museum of Art, University of Connecticut, 1980.

Curtis, Jane and Will, and Frank Lieberman. *Monhegan: The Artists' Island.* Camden, Maine: Down East Books, 1995.

Daniels, Stephen. *Fields of Vision: Landscape Imagery and National Identity in England and the United States.* Princeton, N.J.: Princeton University Press, 1993.

Doezema, Marianne. *George Bellows and Urban America.* New Haven, Conn.: Yale University Press, 1992.

Driscoll, John Paul, and John K. Howat, eds. *John Frederick Kensett: An American Master.* Worcester, Mass.: Worcester Art Museum, 1985.

Edwards, Lee M. *Domestic Bliss: Family Life in American Painting, 1840–1910.* Yonkers, N.Y.: Hudson River Museum, 1986.

Emmet, Alan. *So Fine a Prospect: Historic New England Gardens.* Hanover, N.H.: University Press of New England, 1996.

Fairbrother, Trevor J. *The Bostonians: Painters of an Elegant Age, 1870–1930.* Boston: Museum of Fine Arts, 1986.

Ferber, Linda S. *William Trost Richards: American Landscape and Marine Painter, 1833–1905.* Brooklyn: The Brooklyn Museum, 1973.

Fine, Ruth E. *John Marin.* Washington, D.C.: National Gallery of Art; New York: Abbeville Press, 1990.

Foster, Edward Halsey. *The Civilized Wilderness: Backgrounds to American Romantic Literature, 1817–1860.* New York: The Free Press, 1975.

Gerdts, William H. *American Impressionism.* New York: Abbeville Press, 1984.

———. *Art Across America: Two Centuries of Regional Painting, 1710–1920.* 3 vols. New York: Abbeville Press, 1991.

Glassberg, David. *American Historical Pageantry: The Uses of Tradition in the Early Twentieth Century.* Chapel Hill: University of North Carolina Press, 1990.

Grinnell, Nancy Whipple. *The Light Beyond: Paintings and Prints from the Permanent Collection Depicting Dawn, Twilight, and Moonlight.* Duxbury, Mass.: The Art Complex Museum, 1996.

Harvey, Eleanor Jones. *The Painted Sketch: American Impressions from Nature, 1830–1880.* Dallas: Dallas Museum of Art, 1998.

Hiesinger, Ulrich W. *Childe Hassam: American Impressionist.* New York: Prestel Verlag, 1999.

Hills, Patricia. *The Genre Painting of Eastman Johnson.* New York: Garland Publishing Company, 1977.

Himmelberg, Claudia J. "The Oil Sketches of Albert Bierstadt." Master's thesis, University of California, Santa Barbara, 1978.

Hirschler, Erica E. *Dennis Miller Bunker and His Circle.* Boston: Isabella Stewart Gardner Museum, 1995.

———. *A Studio of Her Own: Women Artists in Boston, 1870–1940.* Boston: Museum of Fine Arts, 2001.

Hobsbawm, Eric, and Terence Ranger, eds. *The Invention of Tradition.* New York: Cambridge University Press, 1983.

Hoppin, Martha. *Eleanor Norcross: Character Is Everything.* Fitchburg, Mass.: Fitchburg Art Museum, 2001.

Horwitz, Howard. *By the Laws of Nature: Form and Value in Nineteenth-Century America.* New York: Oxford University Press, 1991.

Howat, John K., et al. *American Paradise: The World of the Hudson River School.* New York: The Metropolitan Museum of Art, 1987.

Huth, Hans. *Nature and the American: Three Centuries of Changing Attitudes.* Berkeley: University of California Press, 1957.

Hutson, Martha Young. *George Henry Durrie (1820–1863), American Winter Landscapist: Renowned through Currier and Ives.* Santa Barbara, Calif.: Santa Barbara Museum of Art and American Art Review Press, 1978.

Jackson, John Brinckerhoff. *The Necessity for Ruins.* Amherst: University of Massachusetts Press, 1980.

Johns, Elizabeth. *American Genre Painting: The Politics of Everyday Life.* New Haven, Conn.: Yale University Press, 1991.

Judd, Richard W. *Common Lands, Common People: The Origins of Conservation in Northern New England.* Cambridge, Mass.: Harvard University Press, 1997.

Kallir, Jane. *The Artist behind the Myth.* New York: Clarkson Potter for Galerie St. Etienne, 1982.

———. *The World of Grandma Moses.* Washington, D.C.: The International Exhibitions Foundation, 1984.

Kammen, Michael. *Mystic Chords of Memory: The Transformation of Tradition in American Culture.* New York: Knopf, 1991.

Keyes, Donald D. *The White Mountains: Place and Perceptions.* Hanover, N.H.: University Press of New England, 1980.

Larkin, Susan G. *The Cos Cob Art Colony: Impressionists on the Connecticut Shore.* New York: National Academy of Design, 2001.

———. *J. Alden Weir: A Place of His Own.* Storrs: William Benton Museum of Art, University of Connecticut, 1991.

Lears, T. J. Jackson. *No Place of Grace: Antimodernism and the Transformation of American Culture, 1880–1920.* New York: Pantheon Books, 1981.

Levin, Gail. *Edward Hopper.* New York: Knopf, 1995.

———. *Edward Hopper: A Catalogue Raisonné.* New York: Norton, 1995.

Licht, Walter. *Industrializing America: The Nineteenth Century.* Baltimore: Johns Hopkins University Press, 1995.

Lindgren, James. *Preserving Historic New England: Preservation, Progressivism, and the Remaking of Memory.* New York: Oxford University Press, 1995.

Luckey, Laura C., ed. *Highlights from The Bennington Museum.* Shelburne, Vt.: The Bennington Museum, 1989.

MacAdam, Barbara J. *Winter's Promise: Willard Metcalf in Cornish, New Hampshire, 1909–1920.* Hanover, N.H.: Hood Museum of Art, Dartmouth College, 1999.

Marx, Leo. *The Machine in the Garden: Technology and the Pastoral Ideal in America.* New York: Oxford University Press, 1964.

McGrath, Robert L., and Barbara J. MacAdam. *"A Sweet Foretaste of Heaven": Artists in the White Mountains, 1830–1930.* Hanover, N.H.: University Press of New England, 1988.

Miller, Angela. *The Empire of the Eye: Landscape Representation and American Cultural Politics, 1825–1875.* Ithaca, N.Y.: Cornell University Press, 1993.

Miller, David C. ed. *American Iconology: New Approaches to Nineteenth-Century Art and Literature.* New Haven, Conn.: Yale University Press, 1993.

Miller, Perry. *Errand into the Wilderness.* Cambridge, Mass.: Belknap Press of Harvard University Press, 1956.

———. *Nature's Nation.* Cambridge, Mass.: Belknap Press of Harvard University Press, 1967.

Mohlberger, Richard. *Charles Webster Hawthorne.* Chesterfield, Mass.: Chameleon Books, 1999.

Moore, James Collins. "The Storm and the Harvest: The Image of Nature in Mid–Nineteenth Century American Landscape painting." Ph.D. diss., Indiana University, Bloomington, 1974.

Nash, Roderick. *Wilderness and the American Mind.* New Haven, Conn.: Yale University Press, 1973.

New Britain Museum of American Art: Highlights of the Collection, Volume I. New Britain, Conn.: New Britain Museum of American Art and Prestel Verlag, 1999.

New Britain Museum of American Art: Highlights of the Collection, Volume II. New Britain, Conn.: New Britain Museum of American Art and Prestel Verlag, 2003.

Newportraits: Newport Art Museum. Hanover, N.H.: University Press of New England, 2000.

Nicoll, Jessica F. *Allure of the Maine Coast: Robert Henri and His Circle, 1903–1918.* Portland, Maine: Portland Museum of Art, 1995.

Olney, Susan Faxon, et al. *A Circle of Friends: Art Colonies of Cornish and Dublin.* Durham: University Art Galleries, University of New Hampshire, 1985.

Peters, Lisa N. *John Henry Twachtman: An American Impressionist.* Atlanta: High Museum of Art, 1999.

———, and Peter M. Lukehart, eds. *Visions of Home: American Impressionist Images of Suburban Leisure and Country Comfort.* Carlisle, Pa.: Trout Gallery, Dickinson College, 1997.

Piron, Alice Marie O'Mara. "Urban Metaphor in American Art and Literature, 1910–1930." Ph.D. diss., Northwestern University, Evanston, Ill., 1982.

Provincetown Art Association and Museum: The Permanent Collection. Provincetown, Mass.: Provincetown Art Association and Museum, 1999.

Pyne, Kathleen. *Art and the Higher Life: Painting and Evolutionary Thought in Late Nineteenth-Century America.* Austin: University of Texas Press, 1996.

Quick, Michael, et al. *The Paintings of George Bellows.* New York: Harry N. Abrams, 1992.

Reich, Sheldon. *John Marin: A Stylistic Analysis and Catalogue Rasisonné.* Tucson: University of Arizona Press, 1970.

Ricciotti, Dominic. "The Urban Scene: Images of the City in American Painting, 1890–1930." Ph.D. diss., Indiana University, Bloomington, 1977.

Saunders, Richard H., Virginia A. Westbrook, and Nancy Price Graff. *Celebrating Vermont: Myths and Realities.* Middlebury, Vt.: Middlebury College Museum of Art, 1991.

Schmitt, Peter J. *Back to Nature: The Arcadian Myth in Urban America.* New York: Oxford University Press, 1969.

Shi, David E. *Facing Facts: Realism in American Thought and Culture, 1850–1920.* New York: Oxford University Press, 1995.

Smith-Rosenberg, Carroll. *Disorderly Conduct: Visions of Gender in Victorian America.* New York: Oxford University Press, 1986.

Spencer, Harold. *Wilson Henry Irvine and the Poetry of Light.* Old Lyme, Conn.: Lyme Historical Society, 1998.

Stebbins, Theordore E., Jr. *The Life and Work of Martin Johnson Heade: A Critical Analysis and Catalogue Raisonné.* New Haven, Conn.: Yale University Press, 2000.

———. *Martin Johnson Heade.* Boston: Museum of Fine Arts, 1999.

Stein, Roger B. *Seascape and the American Imagination.* New York: Whitney Museum of American Art, 1975.

Stilgoe, John R. *Borderland: Origins of the American Suburb, 1820–1913.* New Haven, Conn.: Yale University Press, 1984.

Sweeney, J. Gray. "A 'Very Peculiar' Picture: Martin J. Heade's *Thunderstorm over Narragansett Bay.*" *Archives of American Art Journal* 28, no. 4 (1988): 2–18.

Truettner, William H., and Roger B. Stein, eds. *Picturing Old New England: Image and Memory.* Washington, D.C.: Smithsonian Museum of American Art, 1999.

Van Buren, Deborah Elizabeth. "The Cornish Colony: Expressions of Attachment to Place." Ph.D. diss., George Washington University, Washington, D.C., 1987.

Van Hook, Bailey. *Angels of Art: Women and Art in American Society, 1876–1914.* University Park: Pennsylvania State University Press, 1996.

Weinberg, H. Barbara, Doreen Bolger, and David Park Curry. *American Impressionism and Realism: The Painting of Modern Life, 1885–1915.* New York: Metropolitan Museum of Art, 1994.

West, Richard V. *"An Enkindled Eye": The Paintings of Rockwell Kent.* Santa Barbara, Calif.: Santa Barbara Museum of Art, 1985.

Wilmerding, John. *American Marine Painting.* New York: Harry N. Abrams, 1987.

———. *Compass and Clock: Defining Moments in American Culture: 1800, 1850, 1900.* New York: Harry N. Abrams, 1999.

———. *Paintings of Fitz Hugh Lane.* Washington, D.C.: National Gallery of Art, 1988.

Library of Congress Cataloging-in-Publication Data

Envisioning New England : treasures from community art museums / edited by Pamela J. Belanger.— 1st ed.

p. cm.

Includes bibliographical references and index.

ISBN 1–58465–380–9 (pbk. : alk. paper)

1. New England—In art—Exhibitions. 2. Painting, American—New England—19th century—Exhibitions. 3. Painting, American—New England—20th century—Exhibitions. 4. Art museums—New England—Exhibitions. I. Belanger, Pamela J.

ND1460.N46E58 2004

758'.174'07474—dc22 2004005928